ROSES

The American Horticultural Society
Illustrated Encyclopedia of Gardening

ROSES

The American Horticultural Society
Mount Vernon, Virginia

For The American Horticultural Society

President
Dr. Gilbert S. Daniels

Technical Advisory Committee
Dr. Henry M. Cathey
Everett Conklin
Mary Stuart Maury

Roses Staff for The Franklin Library/Ortho Books

Editorial Director
Min S. Yee

Supervisory Editor
Lewis P. Lewis

Editor
A. Cort Sinnes

Art Director
John A. Williams

Creative Director
Michael Mendelsohn

Contributing Writer
James K. McNair

Contributing Photographers
William Aplin
Martha Baker
Clyde Childress

Illustrator
Ron Hildebrand

Production Director
Robert Laffler

Production Manager
Renee Guilmette

For Ortho Books

Publisher
Robert L. Iacopi

For The Franklin Library

Publisher
Joseph Sloves

The cover photograph shows two 'Tropicana' roses. This hybrid tea was introduced in 1960, was an All-America Rose Selection in 1963, and was the winner of the American Rose Society Gold Medal Certificate in 1967. Photograph by Rose E. Fujimoto.

Consultants

Harry J. Amling
Auburn University, Auburn, Alabama
Joseph D. Norton
Auburn University, Auburn, Alabama
Henry P. Orr
Auburn University, Auburn, Alabama
Raymond L. Self
Auburn University, Auburn, Alabama
Claron O. Hesse
University of California, Kearney, California
H. P. Olmo
University of California, Davis, California
Perley Payne
University of California, Extension Service,
Santa Clara County, California
Robert G. Platt
University of California, Riverside, California
Alec Hutchinson
Horticultural Research Institute of Ontario, Canada
W. M. Mellenthin
University of Oregon, Mid-Columbia Experiment Station
Robert A. Norton
Northwest Washington Research and Extension Unit
Fay Paquette
Camarillo, California
Robert D. Way
New York State Experiment Station at Geneva

Special Consultants:

R. J. Hutton
Star® Roses, West Grove, Pennsylvania
Douglas Rhymes
Menlo Park, California

Library of Congress Catalog Card Number 80-80415
Printed in the United States of America
12 11 10 9 8

A Special Message from The American Horticultural Society

The American Horticultural Society is particularly pleased to bring you what we feel is the sort of book on roses that has been needed for some time. It takes the mystery out of growing roses and replaces it with all the practical knowledge you need to grow them successfully.

The rose is probably the most fabled and favorite flower in the world, certainly the western world. And it deserves to be. There is nothing quite like it for beauty, elegance, color or fragrance. Unfortunately, perhaps its fame has done the rose a disservice: some people tend to put roses in a special category and think of them as reserved only for those who can afford them and who have a generous amount of time to care for them. Actually, we believe almost everyone should and can have roses. It is true that a good rose bush will cost more than a flat of zinnias or snapdragon plants, but zinnias and snapdragons are annuals and will last for only one season, whereas the rose bush will last for years, even generations, if properly cared for. And not a great deal of care is needed, either. Some roses are difficult to grow, but most are relatively easy. Their delicate appearance belies their actual hardiness. An average of an hour a week, regularly, should be all the time you need to spend caring for 10 to 12 rose bushes.

Here you will learn what a healthy rose bush should look like before you buy it and exactly what to do with it after you have. You will find descriptions of the characteristics, good and bad, of more than 200 of the best roses—miniatures, climbing roses, tea roses, floribundas, old garden roses, grandifloras, tree roses and shrubs. You'll learn which ones are best for which locations, which are the highest rated, and which are All-America Rose Selection winners.

Winter protection and summer cultivation are covered thoroughly. So is how to cut a rose—there is a right way and a wrong way to cut roses, and there are ways to prolong the life of cut roses. All the essentials about the rose are here, and there are even some recipes for cooking and preserving with roses.

This is an invaluable book, and the Society is justly proud of it. We are sure you will be as proud of yourself—and as pleased—once you see the results of what you have learned from it.

Gilbert S. Daniels
President

CONTENTS

  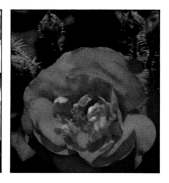

A look at the genus *Rosa* from ancient to modern times. Roses have an interesting history, one that gives even the casual gardener a better idea of how modern hybrids came into being. Old rose varieties represent intrigue and challenge for many gardeners. This chapter explores the rose garden at the Huntington Botanical Gardens, which offers living proof of the long, beautiful history of roses.

This chapter offers basic knowledge about growing all types of roses in all types of situations, where to plant roses, soil-improvement techniques, the best method for planting roses, growing roses in containers, moving established roses and providing roses with the proper fertilizers and amounts of water. Also included is information on miniature roses and how to multiply your rose collection.

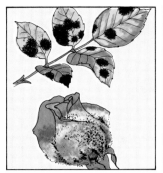 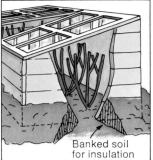 

Banked soil
for insulation

Pests, Protection and Pruning   38

Information in this chapter deals with the basics of rose maintenance: how to minimize pest and disease problems and how to cope with them if they attack; how to prune roses (shrubs, climbers, standards, and old-fashioned varieties)—what equipment is needed, how much and when to prune; protecting roses in areas with severe winters; and reviving old, neglected roses.

Flower description
5" Double (22 petals), light, spicy fragrance
5-6" Double (35-40 petals), moderate fragrance
4½-5" Double (65-70 petals), heavy, tea-rose fragrance, hot climate intensifies color
Large double, slight fragrance

Encyclopedia of Roses   54

Comprehensive charts describe hybrid teas, floribundas, polyanthas, grandifloras, climbers and miniatures. Information includes: the year of the variety's introduction; its color; description of the flower; fragrance and form; foliage description and growth habit of the plant; and current mail-order catalog sources. Check these charts when buying bare-root plants in winter.

Roses in Your Landscape   72

Once roses were thought to belong only in formal gardens, but attitudes have changed over the years. Now you can find roses in every type of landscape imaginable. This chapter describes the basics of designing with roses and shows many different landscape possibilities from various parts of the country. If your outdoor planting space is limited, you can still have a rose garden—in containers and hanging pots.

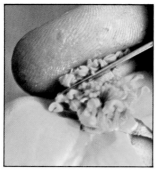  

Creating New Roses 84

Today's roses represent centuries of hybridizing work—work that has combined and recombined genes from countless roses, always hoping to produce improved varieties. This chapter looks at the hybridization process and gives enough detail that you can try your hand at this intriguing hobby. There is technical advice on plant patents, as well as lists of the all-time highest-rated roses.

Cut Roses 106

The enjoyment of many rose growers peaks on the day they bring a beautiful bouquet of freshly cut roses into the house. There are many ways to arrange roses—alone or with other flowers—and this chapter takes a look at a variety of styles. Also included are tips for preserving the life of cut roses and information on the specialized procedure of how best to display roses in competitions and shows.

Preserving Roses 112

There are many ways to keep enjoying roses when the season is over. Preserving roses can be fun for the family, and the results make fine gifts any time of the year. This chapter includes instructions for: drying roses and hips; pressing petals and leaves; making rose potpourri, perfume, soaps and beads, several sachet recipes; and extracting rose oil and rose nectar.

Cooking With Roses 128

The beauty of roses doesn't stop in the garden or in a bouquet—they can be put to good use in the kitchen as well. This chapter contains many little-known recipes for such exotic fare as rose petal jam, English rose wafers and crystallized rose petals. And don't overlook rose hips—the fruit of the rose. They can be used in a number of healthful ways.

Glossary and Final Notes 132

This chapter includes a helpful glossary of terms frequently used in growing roses. Many rose growers become so taken with the subject that they want more information. The American Rose Society provides books and pamphlets for information-hungry growers, as do the other books, catalogs and various Cooperative Extension Services mentioned in this chapter.

OLD AND NEW ROSES

Roses from ancient species to modern hybrids, including descriptions and sources of many that you may want to grow.

The rose, unequaled by any other plant form, has enjoyed universal appeal for centuries. The plants alone are prized as ornamental shrubbery, and the flowers, betokening love and romance, appear on many important occasions of our lives.

Roses have been immortalized in just about every art form. Painters, poets, playwrights, composers, sculptors, craftsmen, and designers have all found a favorite subject in roses. Shakespeare probably spoke for most of the artistic community: "Of all the flowers, methinks a rose is best."

Roses have been important in history since ancient times. Probably the most famous example of this was during the English Wars of the Roses in the 15th century, when the House of York, with a white rose as its emblem, bickered and battled with the House of Lancaster, which had a red rose as its emblem. When Elizabeth of York married the Lancastrian Henry Tudor and they became king and queen, a new hybrid rose blending red and white—the Tudor rose—became the national emblem of England. Many other countries, as well, have used roses on their seals, awards, currency, or postage stamps.

Botanically speaking, all roses belong to the genus *Rosa*, a member of the family Rosaceae. Relatives include almonds, apples, peaches, raspberries, and strawberries. The genus *Rosa* contains about 200 species. Countless crosses of these have produced thousands of hybrids and cultivars.

Roses From B.C. To The Future

At the Huntington Botanical Gardens in San Marino, California, horticulturist John MacGregor has established a very fine collection of roses that repesents the genus from ancient times to the present. A walking tour through his collection will illustrate the history of the rose.

Gallica. We begin at the planting of the oldest cultivated European roses—the Gallica, or French roses. *Rosa gallica* 'Officinalis', often called "the apothecary's rose," predates Christ. The French used it in making medicines and fragrances. The plants are hardy and bloom once each year, in the spring and summer. Flowers may be single, semidouble, or double in form, with 5 to 100 petals each, according to variety. They come in shades of deep red through purple to pink; sometimes they are marbled or striped with white.

Damask. References to these ancient Mediterranean roses appear in old Egyptian records, and they were cultivated in ancient Greece and the Roman Empire. Summer Damask, *R. damascena*, and other varieties are once-blooming; the Autumn Damask, *R. damascena* 'Semperflorens' (*Rosa* x *bifera*), frequently blooms again in the fall. Medium-size double or semidouble flowers grow in large clusters in various shades of pink to white. All are very fragrant. The cultivar 'Trigintipetala' has been grown for centuries to make attar of roses, the purest distillation of rose oils. The plants are hardy and disease-resistant, with tall, thorny, arching, rather weak canes.

Rosa gallica 'Officinalis', B.C.

R. x alba, before 100 A.D.

Rosa × bifera, B.C.

Alba. These roses descend from *Rosa gallica*, crossed with forms of the Dog Rose, *R. canina*. *R. x alba*, which was known before 100 A.D., became very popular during the Renaissance, and it is often found in Italian paintings of the period. The plant is hardy and both pest- and disease-resistant. Flowers are medium in size, delicate, fragrant, and come in shades of pink and white. They bloom once annually, in late spring.

Centifolia. These huge, very fragrant flowers belong to the centifolia roses, which probably were a cross of alba and damask types, produced by Dutch hybridizers before 1500. *R. centifolia* is the "cabbage rose." Usually pink with deep centers, centifolias come in every size, from tiny miniatures to 5-inch globes, and bloom once a year, in late spring or early summer.

Moss. Around 1696, sports of the centifolias known as moss roses appeared. They resemble the centifolias except for a soft, mossy growth covering the calyx and stem. If your fingers touch this growth, they will come away with a sticky, fragrant resin. The plants are quite hardy. Some of the hybrid mosses were bred from the Common Moss and the repeat-blooming damask and China roses.

China and tea. A big boost to European rose development arrived from China in the late 1700s and early 1800s. Forms of *Rosa chinensis*, known as China roses, appeared, followed closely by the first tea rose, *R. odorata*. Chinas have small semidouble red or pink blooms with an occasional white streak, and a peppery fragrance. Tea roses suggest the smell of freshly crushed tea leaves. In size, they are medium to large; in color, pink, cream, and pale yellow. Both are ever-blooming, somewhat tender plants.

The introduction of these ever-blooming roses created much excitement among the breeders, although development was slowed because of the difficulty in crossing the European and China roses, due to genetic differences. However, within a few years, many new forms of roses were created.

Portland. Derived from the Autumn Damasks and Chinas around 1800, these roses were the first of the new China/tea forms to appear.

Bourbon. It was the Bourbon roses that became the most popular new European rose class. They were the result of a cross of Autumn Damask with Pink China. These repeat bloomers have medium, double flowers in shades of pink to red. The plants are compact and vigorous. Hybrid Bourbons are similar, but bloom only once annually.

R. centifolia, before 1500 A.D.

Common moss, about 1696

R. chinensis 'Viridiflora', 1855

Jaune Desprez, Noisette, 1830

R. chinensis 'Mutabilis', before 1914

Hybrid perpetual: Reine des Violettes, 1860

Mabel Morrison, 1878, hybrid perpetual

Variegata di Bologna, Bourbon, 1909

Francis E. Lester, h. musk, 1946

R. chinensis 'Minima', miniature, 1815.

Austrian Copper, R. foetida 'Bicolor', before 1590.

Fru Dagmar Hastrup (Frau Dagmar Hartopp), R. rugosa, 1914.

Soleil d' Or, 1900, founded the Pernetiana class and brought bright yellow to hybrid teas.

Hybrid perpetual. The parentage of hybrid perpetual roses is complex, involving repeated intercrossing among the Portlands, Bourbons, teas, and Chinas. Hybrid perpetuals became very popular during the mid-1800s, when at least 4,000 varieties were introduced. Many are still available and worth growing—they are strong, hardy, vigorous plants that bloom profusely in the spring and repeat modestly through the summer. Their large flowers come in varied forms, in shades of crimson, pink, purple, and white.

Noisette. The first hybrid rose to originate in the United States was the Noisette in the early 1800s. This repeat-blooming, rather tender climber came from the musk rose, R. moschata, crossed with China and tea roses. It blooms in large clusters with soft pastel colors.

Hybrid musk. In the 1920s, the hybrid musks were introduced. Used as either sprawling shrubs or moderate climbers, these are later repeat-blooming versions of Noisettes, crossed with *Rosa multiflora* ramblers. They are very disease resistant and fragrant and will take more cold than the Noisettes.

Hybrid tea. In 1867, J. B. Guillot of France bred 'La France', which at first was considered to be a more compact-growing hybrid perpetual. However, breeding hybrid perpetuals and tea roses produced similar roses with increasing frequency, and soon these were classified as hybrid tea roses.

In 1900, Joseph Pernet-Ducher added the yellow strain of R. foetida to the hybrid teas: his 'Soleil d'Or' offered many new possibilities for hybridizers. For a number of years his brightly colored roses were known as Pernetianas, but by the 1930s this name had gone out of use, and Pernet-Ducher's yellow roses were simply absorbed into the hybrid tea class.

Hybrid teas have undergone constant improvements, becoming *the* rose of the mid-20th century. Flowers are borne singly on long stems or in small clusters. Colors range from whites through lavenders, pinks, yellows, oranges, and reds, with all mixtures and blends in between. Most are fragrant. Plants are grafted onto vigorous shrub rootstock to produce large quantities of salable plants more quickly. They grow from 2 to 6 feet high and bloom continuously.

Polyantha. These roses were introduced in France at about the same time as the hybrid teas. Polyanthas derived mainly from *Rosa multiflora*, crossed with tea and China roses. The low-growing, continuous-blooming plants produce large clusters of small flowers in all rose colors.

Floribunda. Sometimes called hybrid polyanthas, these roses resulted from an early 20th-century cross of polyanthas and hybrid teas. As the name implies, they produce "flowers in abundance." Blooms, resembling hybrid teas in form and color range, are borne in clusters. Most plants are disease resistant, hardy, and low growing.

Grandiflora. About 25 years ago, the grandiflora rose was created as an American classification to designate roses whose characteristics are intermediate between those of hybrid teas and floribundas. The flowers resemble hybrid teas but come in clusters like floribundas, although the plants are larger than floribundas. The growth habit is similar to floribundas, but the plants are generally taller than hybrid teas.

Miniature. Miniature roses came to Europe about 1815 with the introduction of *R. chinensis* 'Minima' (*R. roulettii*). For a while they reigned in France; but tastes changed and they quickly faded into obscurity. Not until the late 1920s was the miniature rediscovered growing in a window in Switzerland. In recent years, these small, tiny-flowered plants have become increasingly popular. Most bloom continuously, and there are varieties in all the colors and forms of hybrid teas, with 5 to 70 petals. They have little or no fragrance.

Climbers. Botanically, climbing roses and ramblers are tall-growing plants (6 to 20 feet) of any one of the other types of roses. Despite their designation, however, they are not true climbers—lacking tendrils or other means with which to attach themselves, they must be tied to a support. (In the wild, their thorns act as tendrils.) These roses may be everblooming or once-blooming each year. They come in a wide range of color, size, and form.

Species and shrub. Species or shrub roses have played a part in the development of modern roses. Many are native species that grow wild in all parts of the Northern Hemisphere. Others have been bred carefully and improved through the years. Most are hardy, often pest- and disease-resistant, and form valuable additions to any landscape. Some of the most beautiful and important ones follow.

R. hugonis, Father Hugo Rose, 1899.

Sweetbrier. *R. eglanteria* (*R. rubiginosa*) and its hybrids have scented foliage reminiscent of ripe apples. The vigorous plants produce 8- to 12-foot arched branches that are quite prickly. Pink, red, or yellow blooms appear once each year in late spring or summer, followed by an abundant crop of colorful hips.

Rugosa. All these derive from *R. rugosa*, and produce large hips that are valuable for their vitamin C. The foliage is rough and ribbed. The plants are very hardy and have fragrant flowers.

Nevada. This modern shrub has big, nearly single blooms in flesh to pure white, sometimes splashed with red.

Chestnut. This rose, *R. roxburghii*, comes from China. Its buds resemble chestnut burrs.

Austrian copper. *R. foetida* 'Bicolor' is a colorful wild shrub that the Moors brought to Europe from Persia in the 13th century.

Father Hugo rose. *R. hugonis*, a beautiful shrub with pale yellow single blossoms, was discovered in China in 1899 by Father Hugh Scallon.

Frühlingsmorgen, 1942.

Kordesii. William Kordes developed an important collection of modern shrubs and semiclimbers in Germany from the sweetbriers and rugosas. The extremely hardy plants have a variety of flower forms and colors.

Plant A New Old Rose

If you've ever been intoxicated by the heady aroma of an old rose, then you'll want at least one heritage plant in your garden. Space does not permit listing all the old roses, species, and newer shrubs available today, but John MacGregor has made a list of some of the best cultivars from each major category of old roses suitable for a beginner's collection. He advises starting with the first one or two cultivars from each group in the accompanying list, if what you want is to establish a broadly representative old rose collection. If you plant all the listed selections from any one group, you will have a good representation of the range of variation within that group.

A Collection For Beginners

Gallica
'Rosa Mundi' (R. gallica 'Versicolor')*
'Tuscany Superb'*
'Belle de Crécy'*
'Charles de Millis'*
'Ipsilanté'*

Damask
R. damascena 'Semperflorens' (Rosa × bifera, Rose of Castile, Autumn Damask)* (R)
'Mme. Hardy'*
'Celsiana'
'Leda' (Painted Damask)
'Marie Louise'

Alba
'Maiden's Blush'
'Koenigin von Daenemark'
'Félicité Parmentier'*
'Mme. Plantier'*
'Celestial'

Centifolia
R. centifolia 'Bullata'
'Petite de Hollande'*
'Rose de Meaux'*
R. centifolia 'Cristata' (Crested Moss)*
'Tour de Malakoff'

Moss Rose
R. centifolia 'Muscosa' (Common Moss)
'Deuil de Paul Fontaine'* (R)
'Salet' (R)
'Henri Martin' (Old Red Moss)
'Gloire des Mousseux'

Tea
'Monsieur Tillier'* (R)
'Catherine Mermet'* (R)
'Maman Cochet'* (R)
'Duchesse de Brabant'* (R)
'Climbing Sombreuil' (R)

Bourbon
'La Reine Victoria' (R)
'Souvenir de la Malmaison'* (R)
'Mme. Ernst Calvat' (R)
'Louise Odier' (R)
'Honorine de Brabant' (R)

China
'Old Blush'* (R)
R. chinesis 'Mutabilis' (R)
'Archduke Charles'* (R)
'Hermosa'* (R)
'Louis Philippe d 'Angers'* (R)

Hybrid Perpetual
'Baronne Prevost' (R)
'Ferdinand Pichard'* (R)
'Paul Neyron'* (R)
'Frau Karl Druschki' (R)
'Heinrich Münch' (R)
'Henry Nevard' (R)
'Baroness Rothschild' (R)
'Reine des Violettes' (R)
'Georg Arends'* (R)
'Ulrich Brunner Fils' (R)

Portland
'Rose du Roi'* (R)
'Comte de Chambord' ('Madam Böll')* (R)
'Jacques Cartier' ('Marquis de Bocella')* (R)

Noisette
'Maréchal Niel' (R)
'Aimée Vibert' (R)

Hybrid Musk
'Buff Beauty' (R)
'Kathleen' (R)
'Prosperity' (R)
'Cornelia' (R)
'Lavender Lassie' (R)

Rugosa
'Fru Dagmar Hastrupp' ('Frau Dagmar Hartopp')* (R)
'Hansa'* (R)
'Sarah Van Fleet'* (R)
'Schneezwerg'* (R)
'Delicata'* (R)

Species
Rosa rubiginosa (Eglantine)
R. foetida 'Bicolor' (Austrian Copper)
R. moyesii
R. hugonis (Father Hugo Rose, Golden Rose of China)
R. rubrifolia (R. glauca)

Shrubs (Species Crosses)
'Harrison's Yellow'
'Golden Wings'* (R)
'Nevada' (R)
'Frühlingsmorgen'
'Stanwell Perpetual'* (R)

*Moderate growers that may easily be kept to a size no larger than the average hybrid tea, suitable to small gardens.
(R) Reliable repeat bloom.

Locating Old Roses

All the roses on the list are available from commercial sources. The following nurseries offer from one or two to many old roses, whose availability varies from year to year. Since there's some disagreement as to correct names, you may have to try several sources to get the exact plant you want. Write for a current listing; see page 140 for names and addresses. Sources: 9, 10, 12, 18, 26, 62, 63, 65, 66, 69, 71, 77, 82, 84, 87, 89, 90, and 92. European nurseries are excellent sources—if you're willing to keep the plants under the two-year quarantine that the law requires.

Most old roses can be propagated easily from cuttings (see pages 34-35) of plants that grow wild or have been planted in old gardens and cemeteries. For additional sources, contact botanical gardens with old rose collections.

Heritage Roses is an organization for those who grow roses of yesterday. A $2 annual membership fee entitles you to four newsletters, plus help in searching for "lost" or hard-to-find roses or books. Write to one of the individuals listed below for further details.

Edith Schurr, 1315 Ninth Avenue North, Edmunds, WA 98020.
Miriam Wilkins, 925 Galvin Drive, El Cerrito, CA 94530.
Carl Cato, Heritage Roses, 5916 Hines Circle, Lynchburg, VA 24502.
Lily Shohan, Heritage Roses, R.D. 1, Clinton Corners, NY 12514.

Bon Bon

A Look Toward The Future

As we've seen, the development of roses has not been static. Who knows what innovations will change our way of thinking once again? Perhaps a new type of rose that will overshadow or improve our present popular classes awaits discovery—indeed, such roses are already under development. And there's even talk of changing the method of classification of existing roses.

Whatever the future brings, we can look forward to more progress in the development of roses—but we must not forget the great roses of yesterday that have inspired artists, lovers, priests, and scientists.

Spellbinder

Jadis

Talisman

Futura

An Aalto freeform vase displays a profusion
of pastel roses in a cool setting for a
summer luncheon.

GROWING ROSES

If you talk to rosarians, read articles on rose culture, check recommendations from state universities, and consult several commercial rose growers' guides, you'll soon discover one fact: There is more than one way to grow a rose.

This section summarizes our research into gardening practices of successful rose-growers. Most of these people realize that other quite successful methods exist—but they still like their own way the most. As with anything—raising a good crop of vegetables, or having a house full of lush greenery—you must find your own way through experience, even a few failures, to a program of rose culture that works best for you.

Roses have a built-in determination to live. It is this "will-to-grow" that accounts for their ability to grow wild in all temperate regions, under a great variety of soil and climatic conditions. They survive all the summer heat, high humidity, dry air, cool fog, strong winds, rains, and countless other weather extremes to which they are subjected. They'll even take quite a lot of abuse from unsympathetic gardeners. But couple their inherent will-to-grow with proper, attentive care, and the rewards will be beautiful.

A rose bush with a full quota of clean leaves and with a constant supply of moisture and nutrients will produce more than twice as many blooms as one that is poorly fed and only partially protected from pests, diseases, and the elements.

Class Them Easy To Grow, And Economical, Too

A lot of people think roses are too tricky and too time-consuming for the average gardener. Certainly, it is true that it takes some effort to grow *good* roses, just as it takes effort to grow *good* tomatoes or *good* marigolds. But the effort is worth it—a healthy plant will continue to produce generous quantities of blooms. You may even find growing roses a lot easier than planting annuals or bulbs, year after year.

It may be a job to water, feed, and protect roses from insects and disease, but if you think of it as a weekly *visit* with your roses, these tasks will turn into pleasant experiences. Think positively; class roses as "easy to grow."

The initial cost of planting roses may seem greater than for seed or bedding plants. But take a long-range view—compare the cost and labor of continually replacing annuals and bulbs with the number of rose blooms produced spring through fall, year after year, and you'll see that roses compensate in every way for the money you invest in them.

Selecting A Site

Roses perform best when they receive full sunshine all day. If this is not possible, plant them where they will get a minimum of 6 hours direct sunlight daily. Morning sun is essential; partial afternoon shade is acceptable.

There should be air movement through the foliage to keep it dry and discourage diseases. Plant the bushes away from large trees or shrub masses, which compete with the roses for nutrients, moisture, and sunlight.

Drainage is a critical factor. If your desired site doesn't drain well, there are several ways to correct that.

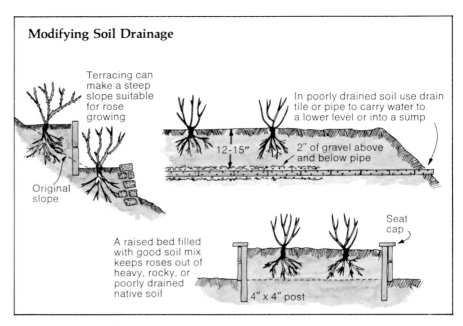

Modifying Soil Drainage

Terracing can make a steep slope suitable for rose growing

Original slope

In poorly drained soil use drain tile or pipe to carry water to a lower level or into a sump

12-15"

2" of gravel above and below pipe

A raised bed filled with good soil mix keeps roses out of heavy, rocky, or poorly drained native soil

Seat cap

4" x 4" post

Some people add several inches of a loose medium such as volcanic cinder or gravel below the bottom level of the prepared soil. Excess water will drain into this loose medium.

Or you can dig a large trench beneath the planting site and bury a drain tile or pipe in coarse gravel. Cover drain openings with asphalt roofing paper to prevent the soil from washing in and clogging the holes. Slant the pipe slightly toward a ditch, storm sewer, or dry well.

An easier solution, however, is to build a raised bed. In very moist areas, build up a bed at least 10 to 15 inches. The side construction can be redwood or masonry framing, old railway ties, or even stone or brick. In addition to giving excellent drainage, raised beds offer a pleasant way to do all the gardening chores. A seat cap lets you sit down beside the roses to work.

Before you plant on a hillside or slope, consider possible erosion problems. Terracing—a modified raised-bed approach—can solve your problem. (See the illustration above for details.)

Roses do well in a wide range of soils, but they prefer loamy soil with high humus content, at least 2 feet deep. A recipe for an ideal growing medium is:

    5 parts (by volume) loamy soil
    4 parts organic matter, such as compost or leaf mold, dehydrated cow manure, peat moss, or shredded bark (all available from garden centers)
    1 part builder's sand

If you use manure, add 3 to 4 pounds of nourishing superphosphate per 100 square feet of soil surface for stronger root development.

If you're planting bushes individually and the soil is good, dig holes 14 to 16 inches wide and 12 to 15 inches deep. Work organic matter and sand into the dug-out soil. Use the same principle for a large bed of roses. Most experts advise that you prepare the soil area 3 to 6 months before you plant the roses.

In cases of extremely poor soil, you may have to remove all existing soil to a depth of 12 to 15 inches and totally replace it with a mixture of good loam, sand, and organic matter.

Roses grow best in a slightly acid soil with a pH of 6.0 to 6.5. Make a soil test to determine the acidity. If the soil is on the alkaline side, add agricultural sulfur at the rate of 2 pounds per 100 square feet, and work into the soil.

It's a good idea to fumigate before you plant if the area has a history of nematodes or some soil-borne disease or has a large weed population. The most satisfactory fumigant for roses is methyl bromide, a gas released under an airtight cover. Your County Extension Agent can provide more information and recommend nearby professional help to apply the fumigant.

When You Plant A Rose

Start with strong-rooted, healthy plants with plump, fresh-looking canes. See pages 36-37 for tips on buying rose bushes.

Container-grown roses can be transplanted into the garden at any time from spring to fall. Often, bare-root roses that don't sell in the spring are canned up for sale later that year. Ask at your nursery for these "leftovers" and you can gain an entire season by planting in fall.

If you're planting in the winter or early spring, get bare-root plants into the ground as early as weather will permit. Early planting gives roots a chance to start growing before the tops break into leaf.

By the time you receive your roses, they probably have dried out somewhat in storage and shipping. To ensure a good start, either bury roots and tops in wet peat moss or sawdust for 2 or 3 days, or completely soak the plants in water overnight. Don't let the roots dry out when you're planting. Carry them to the planting site in a wheelbarrow or bucket half-filled with water.

If you can't plant right away because of weather conditions or your time schedule, wrap the entire soaked plant in wet burlap or newspaper. Store in a dark, cool spot (between 33° and 60° F.). If you still can't plant after a week, soak the bushes again for an hour, rewrap, and store again for up to a week.

If you must keep them even longer, soak them once again and bury them in a trench at a 45-degree angle, covering the tops completely with a few inches of moist soil. They'll hold like this for up to 5 or 6 weeks. Or store them in a large container of moist peat moss in a shaded, protected area.

Planting Times for Packaged or Bare-root Roses are:

Coldest winter temperature	Planting time
10°F.	Any time bushes are dormant
-10°F.	Fall or spring
Below -10°F.	Spring only

There's more than one way to grow a rose. In the lower left, a pick handle is used to compact soil around a transplanted container-grown rose. In the lower right, air pockets in container soil are eliminated by hand.

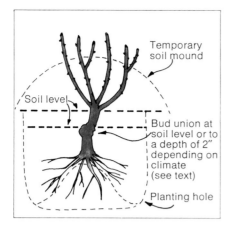

Temporary
soil mound

Soil level

Bud union at
soil level or to
a depth of 2"
depending on
climate
(see text)

Planting hole

Planting Bare-root Roses

After preparing the hole (see next page), prune the soaked rose plant to 3 or 4 strong canes, cutting about 1/4 inch above a good bud. (See pruning, page 46.)

Next, prune the main root pieces to reveal white tissue. These cuts will cause scarring, which will promote increased root production.

Build a cone of soil mixture in the center of the hole to support the spread-out roots, and hold the plant so that the bud union is at the proper ground level. Rosarians, even those within the same region, disagree about the exact placement of the bud union. The general rule of thumb is to place the budhead as much as 2 inches below the soil level in cold-winter areas, and at or slightly above the soil level in mild-winter areas. In mild climates, some rose experts still advocate placing the budhead below the soil level, while others prefer positioning it up to 2 inches above the ground. An exposed budhead encourages basal breaks and makes it easier to control suckers and crown gall. Whatever method you choose, use a pole or shovel handle laid across the planting hole to represent the soil level when you position the plant.

Once you have the plant in position, add about 2/3 of the soil mix, then fill the hole with water. Let it soak in completely. Fill in around the roots with soil mix, and firm gently.

Mound the soil at least 2/3 the height of the plant. (You may have to get extra soil for this.) Moisten again. This mound protects the plant from drying winds and warm sun, and provides enough moisture for the developing plant.

Leave the mound until new growth is 1 or 2 inches long. Then carefully remove it to the ground level and add mulch.

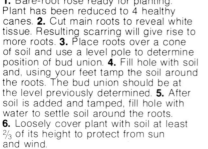

1. Bare-root rose ready for planting. Plant has been reduced to 4 healthy canes. **2.** Cut main roots to reveal white tissue. Resulting scarring will give rise to more roots. **3.** Place roots over a cone of soil and use a level pole to determine position of bud union. **4.** Fill hole with soil and, using your feet tamp the soil around the roots. The bud union should be at the level previously determined. **5.** After soil is added and tamped, fill hole with water to settle soil around the roots. **6.** Loosely cover plant with soil at least ⅔ of its height to protect from sun and wind.

1. Prepare a hole several inches wider and deeper than the container in which the rose is growing.

3. Position the plant in hole and fill in soil. Then tamp down to fill in air pockets.

2. Remove the plant from its container. Leave the soil intact around the plant's roots.

4. Fill basin with water and let the water do the final compacting and irrigation.

Planting Roses Grown In Containers

Dig a hole several inches wider and deeper than the container in which the rose is growing. Mix the soil as outlined on page 20, and place about 6 inches of it in the bottom of the hole.

Remove the plant from the container. If it is a metal can, ask the nursery to slit the sides for you to make removal easier.

Place the rose in the prepared hole at the same level at which it was growing in the container. Add the soil mixture around the root soil.

When the hole is partially filled, compact the surrounding soil to eliminate air pockets (see above). Continue to fill in the hole and pack the soil.

Use water to do the final soil compacting and irrigation. If the rose is growing already, you don't need to mound soil, as you do in bare-root planting.

Add mulch to prevent rapid drying and soil crusting. Keep well watered until established.

Anatomy of a Rose

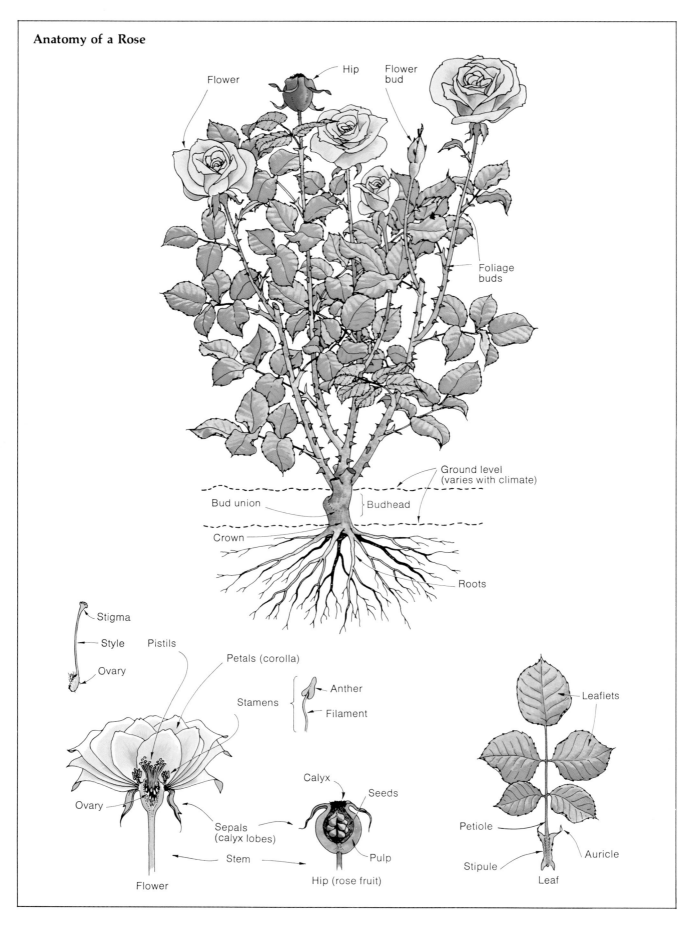

Flower

Hip

Flower bud

Foliage buds

Ground level (varies with climate)

Bud union

Budhead

Crown

Roots

Stigma

Style

Ovary

Pistils

Petals (corolla)

Stamens

Anther

Filament

Ovary

Calyx

Seeds

Sepals (calyx lobes)

Stem

Pulp

Flower

Hip (rose fruit)

Leaflets

Petiole

Auricle

Stipule

Leaf

When You Move A Rose

Transplant roses in the early spring or late fall, when they are as dormant as possible but while the ground is workable.

Prepare the new planting site as you would for planting container-grown roses, making sure the hole you dig is big enough.

Soak the soil around the rose bush overnight so you can dig the plant with as much earth as possible; this minimizes root disturbance. Prune large bushes back to 18 to 24 inches to make handling easier.

Position the plant in the new hole and firm soil around the roots.

Irrigate the plant just as you do for bare-root or container-grown plantings by making a circular dike around the plant.

Label Your Plants

When you buy roses, you also get name tags that are attached with wire, which can damage the cane as it grows. So at planting time remove the wire, attach the label to a stake, and place the stake in the soil near the bush. If you don't like the look of this label, there are many alternatives, plain or decorative.

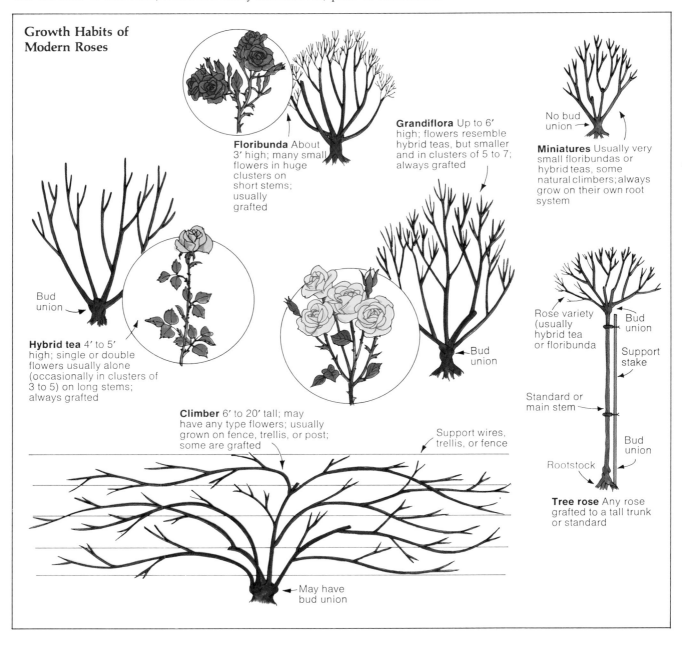

Growth Habits of Modern Roses

Floribunda About 3' high; many small flowers in huge clusters on short stems; usually grafted

Grandiflora Up to 6' high; flowers resemble hybrid teas, but smaller and in clusters of 5 to 7; always grafted

No bud union

Miniatures Usually very small floribundas or hybrid teas, some natural climbers; always grow on their own root system

Bud union

Hybrid tea 4' to 5' high; single or double flowers usually alone (occasionally in clusters of 3 to 5) on long stems; always grafted

Bud union

Climber 6' to 20' tall; may have any type flowers; usually grown on fence, trellis, or post; some are grafted

Support wires, trellis, or fence

May have bud union

Rose variety (usually hybrid tea or floribunda)

Bud union

Support stake

Standard or main stem

Bud union

Rootstock

Tree rose Any rose grafted to a tall trunk or standard

In addition to placing name tags near the plant in the garden, make a diagram of your landscape and write in the names of the roses, the date planted, the source, and any other useful information. This may prove valuable later on, either for you yourself or for the person who may someday buy your home and garden.

Planting And Growing Full-Sized Roses In Containers

Select a container that gives the root system as much freedom as possible. It must be at least 18 inches in diameter and 24 inches deep. A smaller container will make the plant become rootbound and constricted, resulting in defoliation, arrested flower production, or even death.

Wooden tubs and boxes are excellent for roses. Glazed pottery also makes good containers. Porous terra cotta allows moisture to evaporate through the sides, thus keeping the soil cool. Plastic pots are acceptable. Beware of metal containers, however—the summer heat can cook the plant's roots.

Whatever containers you choose, be sure to provide good drainage. Several holes in the bottom are ideal. Cleats, casters, feet, wooden x's, or small pieces of brick underneath the containers help keep the pot from sitting in water. Gravel in the bottom of the pots lets water drain more quickly.

Plant your roses in a growing medium composed of 3 parts sandy loam and 1 part organic matter such as peat moss or leaf mold. You also can get good results with any of the soilless mixes, which you can buy ready-mixed in large bags. If you use the synthetic soils, however, you'll need to be particularly regular with your fertilizing program.

Plant either bare-root bushes or plants already growing in cardboard containers or nursery cans—but roses that have a head start seem to adapt best to container gardening. Perhaps this is because their roots have already adjusted to a confined space, while bare-root plants come directly from fields, where the roots spread out in all directions.

When you're ready to plant, place curved pieces of broken crock over the drainage holes to keep soil from washing through. (If you choose a porous clay pot, soak it for about 30 minutes before planting, so the clay won't rob the roots of soil moisture.) Pour in a few inches of fine gravel, crushed volcanic stone, charcoal, or broken pottery for drainage.

Add a few scoops of soil and set the plant at the proper growing height (see diagram on page 22). Continue adding soil, packing it in well to eliminate air pockets (page 23). Leave a few inches between the soil level and the top of the pot for easier watering. Fill this reservoir with water and let it soak in to finish compacting the soil.

To dress up the container and provide color before the roses start to bloom, you can cover the topsoil with a mulch, plant a shallow-rooted ground cover such as Scotch moss or baby's-tears, or add a few annual transplants.

Care Of Container Plants

Place the container where the bush will get at least 6 hours of direct morning or midday sunlight. If the bush leans toward the sun, find a lighter place. Rotate the pot every few days to keep the plant growing evenly. Keep the plant away from light-colored walls during hot, sunny days—reflected heat can cause foliage burn.

Keep the soil evenly moist at all times during the growing season. Usually, twice-a-week watering is sufficient, but during a hot spell the plant may require daily watering. The more active its growth, the more water it will require.

Fertilizing Container Roses

Feed the plant weekly with liquid plant food. Start with half strength until good growth is established; then increase to full strength, as recommended on the label. If you prefer, apply time-release fertilizers every 3 to 4 months, or use a special combination fetilizer-pesticide product every 6 weeks (see pages 38 and 40).

Planting roses in containers: Pour gravel into bottom of pot. Add some soil, then the plant. Position plant to its proper growing height and add more soil mixture. Irrigate well after planting. Consider annuals around rose for instant color.

When the temperature falls below 28° F., place the plant in an unheated shelter, away from frost and chilling winds. When the bush begins to defoliate, remove all the foliage and bring the pot indoors. Keep the rose away from windows or heat sources where it might be fooled into thinking it's time to start its growth cycle again. Water occasionally during dormancy, just enough so the soil doesn't dry out. Do not feed. After the danger of frost is over, move the pot outdoors again. Prune lightly to initiate new growth.

In mild areas where the temperature stays above 28° F., the plant can live outdoors all year. Cut back its water and eliminate feeding during winter months to induce dormancy.

Eliminating Weeds, Plus...

The soil around roses requires just enough cultivation to eliminate weeds and prevent tight surface crusts from forming. Cultivating soil to a very shallow level will avoid injury to roots that may be growing close to the surface. Deep cultivation can destroy feeder roots.

Pulling weeds by hand or cutting them at soil surface can eliminate cultivation, if there's no problem with soil crusting.

If you use a chemical weed control, be sure to follow the directions on the manufacturer's label. For easiest care, combine chemical weed control, nutrients, and pesticides in one application of systemic rose care (see pages 38 and 40). Be sure to spray according to the manufacturer's suggested distances from fruit trees and vegetable gardens.

Mulches Provide The Plus

The role of mulching in rose culture cannot be overemphasized. Look at what mulch does for you:

☐ Eliminates continual cultivation of soil.
☐ Controls weeds.
☐ Retains soil moisture.
☐ Keeps soil temperature more even in both summer and winter.
☐ Cuts down damage from alternate freezing and thawing of winter soil.
☐ Prevents soil crusting and erosion.
☐ Renews and rebuilds humus content of soils (if the mulch is organic).
☐ Encourages root growth.
☐ Activates helpful earthworms and bacteria in the soil.
☐ Completes the landscape design with a neat, manicured look.

After a new planting, apply mulch to a depth of 2 to 4 inches. Mulch used to be put out and taken up before and after every growing season, but modern tests have proven the advantage of keeping the mulch in place all year. As organic mulches decay into the soil, add new applications.

If there has been a disease problem, remove all the old mulch and replace it with clean, fresh material in early fall.

There's a wide range of mulching materials to choose from. Which you choose depends on availability, cost, ease of handling, and personal preference.

If there's danger of bringing in weed seed along with the organic mulch materials, either select another mulch or fumigate the organic materials before applying (see page 20).

Our chart describing various mulches (see page 28) includes both their advantages and their disadvantages.

Providing Fuel For Rose Productivity

The rose is a high-powered manufacturing plant that needs a continuous supply of water and plenty of nutrients in order to produce flowers.

Your plant must have a profusion of leaves to bear lots of beautiful roses. It takes 25 to 35 perfect leaves to create one perfect rosebud and bring it into bloom. The leaves use sunlight to convert nutrients and water into fuel for growth and flower production.

A most attractive mulch of bark chips around a freshly planted rose.

Mulching Material

Material	Comments
Bark	Available commercially in chip form or finely ground. Very attractive and long lasting.
Buckwheat hulls	Very attractive, but tend to scatter in windy locations.
Cotton screenings, peanut hulls, shredded tobacco stems	Fairly durable. Supply plant nutrients and improve soil structure. Obtainable from processing plants and mills.
Grass clippings or hay	Probably the most available mulch, but unattractive. Let dry before spreading. Repeated use builds up reserve of available nutrients which lasts for years.
Gravel or stone chips	Not too attractive with roses. Extremely durable, holds down weeds, but does not supply plant nutrients or humus.
Ground corn cobs	Excellent for improving soil structure.
Mushroom compost (spent)	This material is often available in areas where commercial mushrooms are produced. It is usually inexpensive, with a good color that blends into the landscape.
Newspaper	Readily available. Can be used shredded or in sheets, held in place by rocks, bricks, or soil. Cover with more attractive material. Builds humus, and ink contains beneficial trace elements.
Peat moss	Attractive at first, tends to lose esthetic appeal wih age. Available, but expensive for large areas. Compacts and sheds rain water. Should be kept moist at all times.
Pecan hulls	Extremely durable, availability limited.
Pine needles	Will not mat down. Fairly durable. Potential fire hazard.
Plastic film	Excellent mulch, but unattractive. Can be covered with thin layer of bark. Punch holes for penetration of water. Eliminates weeds entirely.
Rotted manure	May contain weed seeds.
Sawdust, wood chips or shavings	Low in plant nutrients, decompose slowly, tend to pack down. Rose foliage may yellow; additional nitrogen will correct the problem. Well-rotted material preferred. Can be fresh if nitrate of ammonia or nitrate of soda is supplemented at the rate of one pound per 100 square feet. Keep away from building foundations; may attract termites.
Straw	Long-lasting. Depletes nitrogen, but furnishes considerable potassium.
Tree leaves (whole or shredded)	Excellent source of humus. Rot rapidly, high in nutrients.

You Can't Give A Rose Too Much Water

One thing rose people do agree on is that you can't give a rose too much water. But a rose will not tolerate wet feet! Drainage must be excellent. (See page 20.)

Rose foliage will wilt if water is insufficient. Always water enough to keep the moisture at a level where the leaves will be distended with water, or "moisture-turgid." Don't let the rose wilt.

Unfortunately, we can't tell you exactly how much or how often to water. These standards depend on soil type, climate, and the growth stage of the rose. Your rose will need more water: when the soil is loose and sandy or heavily compacted; when the air is hot and dry; or when new plants are developing.

Normally, a rose should receive the equivalent of 1 inch of rainfall per week, all at one time, starting in early spring and continuing through fall. Hot and dry weather may call for watering every 3 or 4 days, more often during drought. Even when rainfall is plentiful, porous soils benefit from additional deep soakings.

In the early spring, water your roses from overhead to prevent the canes from drying while they develop. When foliage growth begins, keep the water away from the leaves; instead, apply it directly to the soil for best results.

Water well when you water, soaking the soil to a depth of 8 to 10 inches. A light sprinkling is worse than no water at all. Frequent light applications create shallow root systems and increased susceptibility to drought conditions.

Since rosarians cannot agree on the correct method of watering, you have a choice—you can sprinkle or use one of several forms of irrigation.

Some people build a basin or dike around the entire bed; others prefer a basin around each rose bush. If you opt for either of these methods, flood the basin with water, which slowly will soak into the soil. This works well in dry-summer regions.

The most efficient system seems to be slow-drip irrigation at the base of the

Rose Plant Watering

Plastic (PVC) pipe, laid on the ground with a hole at each bush, waters the basins efficiently...

PVC pipe may be set a couple of inches beneath the soil surface and near each rose bush, where special risers dispense water right at the roots

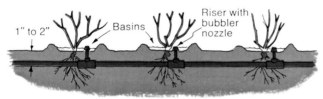

1" to 2"   Basins   Riser with bubbler nozzle

Deep root soaking of an entire rose bed may be accomplished by installing this system before you plant

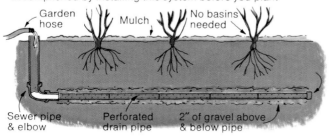

Garden hose   Mulch   No basins needed

Sewer pipe & elbow   Perforated drain pipe   2" of gravel above & below pipe

... or you may use spaghetti tubes that extend from a pipe near the center of the bed. Pipes may be hidden by mulch.

This spaghetti tube soaker may be attached to a regular garden hose for a temporary system that will water 6 rose bushes. Tubes are 4', 8', and 12' long

plants. Using a heavy stream of water from a hose is wasteful—most of it runs off, and what remains penetrates the soil only a few inches. A soaker hose, or one of the methods illustrated above, can provide deep soaking to moisten the soil to the required depth. And because this system will not wet the foliage or spread the mulch, the chances of disease will be reduced. A soaker hose saves you time, energy, and even money, because in the long run you use less water.

If you do choose to sprinkle, however, water early in the morning so the leaves can dry before they are exposed to the hot midday sun. Be sure the sprinkler runs for a long enough time to soak the water 8 to 10 inches deep into the soil. This method will require you to make more frequent application of fungicides to guard your roses against mildew and blackspot.

Growing roses in well-defined beds makes it easy to irrigate, fertilize, and keep the area weed-free.

Choose Rose Food From A Varied Menu

Since a rose is a heavy user of nutrients, it needs regular applications of fertilizer for optimum growth. The rate, frequency, and kind of fertilizer depend on the type of soil. As for frequency, plants in sandy soils benefit from frequent applications; those in heavy soils may not need as much. As for kind, a soil test can help determine the particular balance of nitrogen, phosphorus, and potassium you need. Or check with your County Extension Agent or nurseryman for recommended fertilizer ratio and application rates for your local area.

Wait until your newly planted bushes have become established—about 3 or 4 weeks after planting—before you begin your fertilizer program.

Some rose people advocate 3 applications per year for hybrid teas, grandifloras, and floribundas:

Early spring, just after pruning, when the bush begins to leaf out.

Early summer, when the plant is beginning to flower.

Late summer, to carry the plant on through fall. In warm coastal areas, your plants may need an additional application in the fall.

(A single application per year, early in spring before the leaves come out, usually is enough for climbers and shrub species.)

Most rosarians agree that all types of roses need more frequent applications, beginning in early spring as the bush puts out leaves, then continuing every 6 weeks, or even once each month, through late summer.

You can choose from several types of fertilizers, both organic and inorganic. Most people opt for the inorganic because of its controlled reliability, specific formulation for roses, and easy availability.

Liquid food is preferred and used exclusively by quite a few rosarians. However, many more rose experts like to apply liquid to newly planted bushes every 2 to 3 weeks until the plant is established, and then to switch to granular fertilizers for a regular diet.

When using liquid rose food, follow the label directions for mixing. Unless the product is specifically recommended for foliar feeding, wash off any remaining liquid fertilizer from the foliage.

Ingredients in a Balanced Plant Diet

Elements	Contributions	Signs of Malnutrition
Primary elements		
Nitrogen	Promotes green growth—good canes, stems, leaves. (Too much overstimulates foliage growth at expense of flowers.)	Yellow leaves No new growth Failure of buds to open Small, pale flowers
Phosphorus	Good root growth and flower production	Dull green foliage Falling leaves Weak stems Abnormal root system Slow-to-open buds
Potassium	Vigorous growth	Yellow leaf margins, turning brown Weak stems Underdeveloped buds
Secondary elements		
Calcium	Growth of plant cells and good roots	Deformed growth and abnormal root development
Magnesium	Good growth	Mature yellow leaves, tinged maroon
Sulfur	Green growth	Yellowing of new leaves
Trace elements		
Boron	Good form	Small, curled, and scorched leaves Dead terminal buds
Chlorine	Good growth	Malformed foliage
Copper	Good growth	Poorly developed tips
Iron	Keeps plants green	Yellow foliage
Manganese	Increases nitrogen	Pale mottling of leaves
Molybdenum	Good growth	Poorly developed leaves
Zinc	Good growth	Malformed growth

Note: Malnutrition, deficiency, or overabundance do not occur in plants that are given properly balanced fertilizers for the particular soil.

Follow a routine spraying program during growing season or spray to combat invasions.

In foliar feeding, food is sprayed directly onto the foliage, which uses it immediately. Thus the root system of distribution is bypassed. Some rose growers combine foliar feeding with their regular pesticide spraying every 2 weeks. Adding some foliar food just before the peak of the blooming season can produce roses of exhibition quality. However, do not apply foliar food in hot weather.

If you select granular fertilizers, be sure to wet the soil first. Apply the fertilizer about 6 inches away from the main stem. Distribute the prescribed amount uniformly out beyond the branch spread, and work into the surface of the soil or mulch. Water well after applying.

You can use granular fertilizers alone or in combination with systemic pesticides formulated for use every 6 weeks during growing season, as described on pages 38 and 40.

In fertilizing, the most important thing is to maintain a consistent program. You like your meals on time when you're hungry; so does the rose. Whichever type of fertilizer you choose, pay close attention to the label directions. Over-fertilizing can cause damage by leaving salt deposits in the soil that cause stunted growth, off-color foliage, and death of new foliage. Water heavily to put the salts in suspension; then follow with another heavy watering to leach them out of the soil.

Miniature Roses Indoors And Outdoors

You can easily grow miniature roses around the house all year long. Outdoors, plant them in the ground or in containers—even in hanging baskets. Indoors, grow them in a sunny window or under artificial lighting.

Potted miniatures adapt well to mobile gardening. Grow them in a favorable outdoor environment in warm seasons, then bring them indoors and enjoy the blooms. When the flowers fade, return the plants to the garden to rebloom. Or put them outdoors, when weather permits, then bring them inside for a winter garden. Try growing them under lights all year. When the plants bloom, place them anywhere you want and enjoy the flowers for a few days.

Outdoor Culture

Caring for small varieties differs only slightly from caring for large roses. Since small roses grow on their own roots, you don't have to worry about bud unions when you plant. Whether you plant in a pot or in the ground, set the rose bush slightly deeper into the soil than it originally grew.

Most varieties should be spaced about 10 to 12 inches apart. Make sure the roses are separated from large plants that can rob them of much-needed sunshine and moisture.

When you read catalog descriptions of miniature plant sizes, remember that these are based on indoor or greenhouse pot culture, where size is regulated by the restricted root growth. Although the flowers remain tiny, many of the miniature plants will grow quite large when planted in the ground, especially in temperate climates. If you want to keep the bushes small, you'll need to prune them back severely.

Pruning is easy. In the spring, just clip the plant back into the desired shape, as you would boxwood, and shake out the clippings. You can prune miniatures back to 1/2 their size.

These little plants are more cold resistant than most hybrid teas or other garden roses, and they require little winter protection. In warm climates, they even bloom all year.

Miniatures can be bedded together or share containers with a host of small companions. Here are only a few suggestions:

Annuals—alyssum, calendula, lobelia, marigold, fairy primrose, and viola;
Bulbs—crocus, grape-hyacinth, miniature tulip and iris, and narcissus;
Groundcovers—small-leaved ivy, baby's-tears, and sedum;
Herbs—basil, oregano, and parsley;
Vegetables—garlic, kale, leaf lettuce, and Swiss chard;
Other small plants—boxwood and ferns.

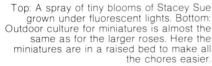

Top: A spray of tiny blooms of Stacey Sue grown under fluorescent lights. Bottom: Outdoor culture for miniatures is almost the same as for the larger roses. Here the miniatures are in a raised bed to make all the chores easier.

Year-Round Indoor Roses

The miniatures will bloom indoors all year, taking only a 2-month rest. You can expect a cycle of blooms every 6 to 8 weeks. With roses potted up at various times, it's possible to have continual flowering. Select compact, low-growing varieties for indoor use.

Plant in a 4- to 8-inch pot with a mixture of equal parts sterilized garden soil, peat moss (or other organic humus), and coarse sand (or perlite). Be sure the container has excellent drainage. Immerse the freshly planted rose in water just over the pot rim, until all bubbling stops.

After planting and soaking, put the bush on a cool porch, in a coldframe, or a cool, protected outdoor area where it can acclimate itself for 2 to 4 weeks. When renewed growth begins, place the plant indoors in a sunny window.

Keep the soil evenly moist, never soggy wet. Occasionally let the surface dry out completely; then water well from the top of the pot. Yellow leaves indicate improper drainage or too much water.

Yellow leaves can also indicate that the surrounding air is too dry. Miniature roses like more moisture than the average house provides. Build up the humidity by keeping the plant on a tray filled with pebbles or sand. Maintain some water in the bottom of the tray, but don't let it get so deep that it reaches the bottom of the pot. Wash the foliage in the sink routinely—this will help add moisture, remove any residues from sprays or household grease, and keep the insect population under control.

Grow miniatures on a moist pebble tray in a sunny window.

Feed with a houseplant fertilizer monthly. Follow a preventive spray program, as for regular outdoor roses, to control diseases and pests (see pages 40-43). The worst enemy of miniature roses is spider mite. Keep an eye out and provide early treatment.

Some growers suggest that you give your miniatures an annual 8-weeks' rest during the hottest summer months. To accomplish this, place the plant in the hydrator (vegetable bin) of a refrigerator. Then, when the forced dormancy period is over, cut the plant back to 1/2 its size and resume normal care.

Prune the plant any time you wish to keep it to the desired shape and size. Cut back to about 1/3 its height with sharp, clean shears, just above a 5-leaflet leaf. Pinch or trim new shoots to induce branching. Keep spent blooms pinched off. You may need to repot miniatures each year, along with other plants grown indoors.

Roses Under Man-Made Sun

Miniature roses are good candidates for light gardening. They remain compact, since they never have to reach for the light source, and they're covered with blooms in 6- to 8-week cycles most of the year.

Place the plants under a bright light. Keep the light source 10 to 12 inches above the top of the rose. Set the lights on a timer to establish a controlled routine of 16 to 18 hours of light per day.

You can choose from among many types of lighting fixtures and bulbs. Many people favor the old reliable formula of equal portions of fluorescent tubes and incandescent bulbs. Or you can use two cool white fluorescent tubes; one cool and one warm tube; or the full-spectrum fluorescents, such as Agro-lite, Vita-lite, or Duro-lite, that are designed for plant growth.

Multiply Your Rose Collection

It's fairly easy to propagate new rose bushes from existing plants. Not only do you save money by duplicating roses that you have grown already, but also it's fun to watch the new plant emerge and develop. You can share cuttings or seed-

Softwood Stem Cuttings

This is the easy way to reproduce favorite plants. It is especially successful with old and shrub roses.

Make 6- to 8-inch cuttings when the bloom has faded. Remove the flower, along with a few inches of the top stem. Leave only 1 or 2 leaves at the top. Dip the bottom end into a root hormone stimulant to speed up root development.

Set cuttings, immersed to 1/2 their length, into a damp growing medium composed of equal parts sand (or perlite) and peat moss (or vermiculite).

Insert 2 tall stakes into the soil to support a plastic bag. Seal the bag to create a greenhouselike climate. Store it in a bright place, away from direct sunlight.

Remove the bag when new growth begins (usually 5 to 8 weeks). Transplant each cutting to a pot, or to the garden where it will get partial shade for a couple of weeks. See page 140 for a list of mail-order nurseries that offer retail catalogs. Write for those that offer the types of roses that interest you. You don't necessarily have to order from nearby nurseries; the origin of the plant isn't as important as its quality.

The numbers following the company names are from the list of seed and nursery suppliers; they correspond to the source column on the charts beginning on page 56.

Let the top 2 leaves remain...

Pull off lower leaves, being careful not to damage buds

Set cuttings into damp soil mix

Seal in a plastic bag until new shoots appear— in about 5 to 8 weeks

Transplant to a pot or planter, or its own place in your rose garden

lings with friends or other rosarians to build up a collection of hard-to-find roses. Just be sure that any plants you reproduce vegetatively (from cuttings) are non-patented roses (see pages 88-89). You don't have to worry about this when starting roses from seed, however.

Growing From Seed

Seed propagation can be practiced with species roses, or with the new seeds resulting from hybridization (see page 86-88).

Select a shallow tray or flat with several drainage holes; fill it with fine sand or vermiculite. Shell the seeds and plant them 1/2 inch deep. Water thoroughly. Keep the sprouting medium warm (around 55-60°F.) and moist, never soggy wet. Provide no light until the seeds begin to germinate; then give 16 hours of light a day.

Germination will begin soon, and it will continue for 2 or 3 months. Seedlings emerge with a bent neck and straighten out in a few days. Cotyledons (seed leaves) will stretch out horizontally and turn green.

Then they are ready to be transplanted to a potting medium. The American Rose Society recommends a medium composed of equal parts of sterilized topsoil, perlite, and peat moss. To each bushel of the mixture, add 1 cup dolomite lime, 1 cup superphosphate, 1 cup rose food, and 1 cup 50 percent Captan.

Transplant the tiny seedlings into well-drained, large plastic or metal pans or flats filled with the growing medium. Give them 16 hours of good light per day in a warm place (70°F.). Fluorescent fixtures give excellent, controlled lighting for growing the seedlings.

Water sparingly. Blot off any water that remains on the leaves. Allow plenty of ventilation. After the first true leaves form, either put them into 3-inch pots with the same soil mixture as before, continue growing them in flats, or transplant them into the garden. Seedlings may bloom when they are several months old.

Bud the seedlings that do well onto sturdy rootstock. Eliminate or recross the less-hardy seedlings with other hybrids.

This recently emerged rose seedling holds within it all the potential for many years of beautiful flowers.

Hardwood Cuttings

Here's a simple way to reproduce old bush and climbing roses.

In late fall or early winter, cut mature canes of the current season's growth into 5- to 6-inch lengths. Bury them vertically in a box of sand or peat moss. Store in a cool place (32-50°F.). Keep moist through winter. The plants should be ready to put out into the garden in spring.

You can also treat them like softwood cuttings, but do not place them under a plastic cover. Keep soil medium moist and cool. A successful method of propagating old roses in warm climates (only) relies on refrigeration. Make a 5- to 6-inch cutting, wrap it in plastic, and put in refrigerator to callous. After a few weeks, pot it in sand and perlite, peat moss, or a soilless medium, and put it inside a plastic bag. Place the bagged pot in the refrigerator for 2 or 3 months. Then place it in filtered sunlight and begin watering.

Budding For Vigorous Growth

Budding or bud-grafting is the common propagation method for hybrid roses —it gives them a more vigorous root system. Budding is an inexpensive way to duplicate plants, since each cane cutting (budwood) will have at least 4 buds, each capable of producing a new plant.

In the fall or winter, select a healthy piece of rootstock and root 8- to 10-inch cuttings, leaving only the top 2 buds to develop. *Rosa multiflora* and 'Dr. Huey' are the most commonly used plants; any sturdy shrub or old rose that roots easily will do.

The following spring or summer, cut a piece of budwood from the hybrid rose or new seedling. Wrap it in plastic and age it in the refrigerator for a few weeks. Then, using a small, sharp knife, cut a scion (a single bud and a small portion of the surrounding bark) from the budwood.

Cut a T-shaped opening in the outer skin of the rooted stock cane, below the foliage. Insert the bud or scion into the T-cut on the rootstock plant. Be sure that the bud goes into the cut all the way.

Bind the bud into the grafting cut with a piece of budding rubber or a plastic bud cover (your County Extension Service can recommend local sources). Then break the top of the rootstock between the bud graft and the foliage. This will encourage proper development of the bud union. The band will rot after a few weeks, leaving the bud grafted onto the rootstock. Keep the soil moist and provide filtered sunlight.

By the following spring, if the grafted bud takes, you can expect healthy foliage. At that time, completely remove the greenery of the rootstock, including any rootstock growth buds (the source of suckers). Vigorous new roots support the young plant as it continues to grow and develop.

Buy Plants Cautiously

You can buy rose plants either bare-root (wrapped and packaged, loose, or in plantable boxes) or growing in containers (often with full growth and sometimes flowers). Either type of plant will produce good roses. Container-grown bushes may give you fewer problems at planting time, but bare-root plants will come in a wider selection of varieties.

1. Cut a scion from a piece of budwood. **2.** Make a T-cut in the stem of rootstock. **3.** Insert the hybrid bud inside rootstock. **4.** Bind the bud onto the rootstock stem. **5.** Remove stock top when a hybrid growth starts.

Nurseries and garden centers offer bare-root roses or container-grown plants, often in bloom.

Roses are graded by a rating system—1, 1½, and 2—based on size and number of canes. If you're willing to pay the price for the best possible blooms, insist on Grade No. 1 plants with 3 or 4 heavy canes at least 3/8 inch in diameter. Hybrid teas should be 18 inches in height; floribundas should be 15 inches. While it's possible that grade 1½ plants may catch up after a few seasons of growth, you will miss those first years of good bloom quality that you get with grade 1. Inferior grades will not give you specimen flowers.

Purchase plants from well-known mail-order houses or established garden centers or nurseries. Buy from the people who sell roses year after year and stand behind the quality of their plants. Avoid bargains. Since your investment of time and energy in each rose will be considerable, it's worth spending the little extra money for quality plants.

Most bare-root roses are grown in California, where the environment is conducive to growing top-grade plants that are just as hardy (or perhaps hardier) in cold climates as roses grown in northern fields.

The plants are harvested when they are dormant, kept under ideal conditions, and shipped to retailers or directly to you at the right planting time for your local climatic conditions.

Fresh plants that have been kept moist by a knowledgeable nurseryperson or sent directly from a mail-order supplier will perform better than bare-root roses that have been held in dry overheated stores for long periods. It's all right to buy plants from retail stores—but only if the stock has been kept dormant and protected from drying out.

When you shop for plants, examine the rose bush to be sure the wood is not dry and shriveled. Look for a well-shaped plant that has neither deformed growth nor abnormal swellings nor discolorations on canes or roots—these may be symptoms of disease. The bark on the canes should be firm, plump, and green. The root system should be sturdy and fibrous and have several firm, well-branched roots.

PESTS, PROTECTION AND PRUNING

It is generally agreed that maintaining well-pruned and pest-free plants is especially important in growing roses—the subject of winter protection is a little more controversial.

Take a leisurely walk through your garden every few days and enjoy the beautiful rewards of your labor. At the same time, keep an eye out for early signs of trouble, such as wilted foliage, deformed flower buds, or spots on leaves.

If you discover any such symptoms, don't jump to the conclusion that your garden is disease- or pest-ridden (unless, of course, you actually find some insects). Instead, take time to diagnose the problem. Remember that many plant troubles can be caused by poor gardening practices. Not enough water can cause wilt; too much water can cause rot; alkaline soil can cause yellow leaves. Make sure the problem is not a cultural one before you spray unnecessarily.

Prevention Is The Key Word

Remember, a rose that is growing vigorously can withstand more injury from unwanted invaders than can a rose that is under stress from lack of water or nutrients.

You can prevent some diseases simply by watering correctly (see page 29). Avoid watering the entire rose bush; this can cause mildew. Water only the soil underneath the bush. When using the hose, avoid splattering soil or mulch; this spreads powdery mildew or blackspot.

You can minimize losses from diseases by obtaining the best-quality rose plants—those that show no abnormal swellings on the roots or crowns and are free of discolored areas on stems. Buy from reliable sources who guarantee their product to be disease-free. Choose cultivars with built-in disease resistance. There are many to choose from.

Practice maintenance pruning. Remove all canes showing cankers as soon as you detect them. And be sure to destroy the prunings. As soon as you notice them, remove and destroy individual leaves bearing black spots.

Don't forget a winter cleanup. If you do a thorough cleanup job when your roses are dormant, you'll have fewer insects and disease organisms to combat when the new leaves unfurl in the spring. To keep rust and blackspot from carrying over from year to year, strip all leaves from your bushes. Rake up any leaves that have fallen, and burn or dump them in the garbage can. Spray the canes, as well as the soil or mulch beneath the canes, with a specially formulated dormant spray and thoroughly drench twigs and canes.

Set up a regular spray schedule for disease and pest control during the growing season. If you apply preventive spray or dust regularly and follow that with a multipurpose pesticide application every couple of weeks during the growing season, you may never even see any pests or evidence of disease. On the average, this takes about an hour per week to care for most rose gardens.

Systemics provide an alternative approach to spraying. A systemic applied to the soil gives the plant the power to protect itself from its worst enemies. And when you use products that combine nutrients with pesticides, you save even more time and energy.

Mildew

If you apply a systemic every 6 weeks, you won't have to do routine spraying for the normal attacks of aphids, spider mites, white flies, leafmining insects, leafhoppers and other sucking types. A systemic gives the plant internal protection that rain or water from sprinklers cannot wash off, while allowing beneficial insects such as ladybugs and bees to go unharmed.

However, sometimes you may be faced with an invasion of pests and in need of additional help. Act quickly: spray or dust at the very first sign of attack. If you get the first aphids, the first brood of beetles, or the first invasion of thrips, you'll minimize your use of sprays and damage to the plants.

Using Chemical Controls

When you do use sprays, let your common sense guide you. And use the following pointers to learn how to use modern science's most potent methods of dealing with garden problems.

☐ Observe all directions and precautions on pesticide labels. They are there for your benefit.

☐ Store all chemical products behind locked doors, in their original containers with labels intact. Keep them away from foodstuffs and out of the reach of children and pets.

☐ Use pesticides at correct dosages and intervals to avoid unnecessary residues and injury to plants and animals. Never use a stronger spray than the manufacturer recommends. Experts have formulated these sprays carefully to do the most effective job.

☐ Mix chemicals in an open area. Spray on calm days, to prevent drifts. Work on the windward side when applying. Clothe yourself from head to toe when spraying, and avoid prolonged inhalation of any chemical.

☐ Wrap surplus pesticides and used containers in paper and place in garbage cans. This will keep contamination of water and other hazards from occurring.

☐ After handling pesticides, be sure to wash before you eat, drink, or smoke.

There are now federal restrictions on the use of certain chemical controls. If in doubt, check your state and local regulations.

Use Your County Agent

Don't hesitate to ask your local County Extension Service for help and recommendations in combating pests and diseases. Your local agent keeps abreast of current studies going on at your state university research stations, and can answer questions on problems peculiar to your area.

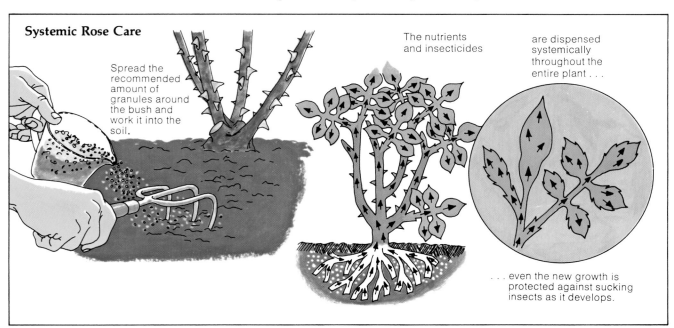

Systemic Rose Care

Spread the recommended amount of granules around the bush and work it into the soil.

The nutrients and insecticides are dispensed systemically throughout the entire plant . . .

. . . even the new growth is protected against sucking insects as it develops.

Let Nature Help

In addition to using pesticides, you might want to call on a couple of nature's helpers to help you outsmart rose spoilers. Beneficial predatory insects such as ladybug beetles, praying mantis, Trichogramma wasps, and lacewings can help keep the population of aphids and other pests under control. You can leave a couple of bushes unsprayed as a haven for these good guys, or rely on systemic pesticides applied to the soil and taken up in the sap stream, since these systemics do not harm the helpful insects.

Birds can be a menace to the vegetable garden or fruit orchard, but they can be a delightful asset to the rose garden. Insect-eating species include bluebirds, chickadees, mockingbirds, orioles, robins, wrens, and warblers. Encourage their visits by hanging bird feeders near your roses.

The charts on the next two pages describe specific rose trouble symptoms, identify the problem, and suggest some solutions.

Other Pests

Ants often follow the paths of aphids to eat the sticky honey residue left by them. They may build nests in the ground, which can disturb the rose roots. Use Diazinon to eradicate.

Deer love to feed on tender young rose shoots. Garden centers have repellents that you can spray on foliage or apply to the soil around the planting area.

Leafcutter bees make perfect circles and ovals in rose leaves during the summer. Unfortunately, there's no control for this leaf damage—since the bee doesn't eat the cut-out portion but uses it to line its nests, poisons are not effective. And even if they were, we wouldn't want to harm these bees that are integral in natural pollination. The solution? Cut out any wilted or dying shoots that the bees may have used as nesting material.

Moles, searching for food, can disturb roots with their tunneling, causing rose plants to grow unhealthily or even die. You can buy mole traps, or you can treat the soil with a soil insecticide like Diazinon to kill many of the soil insects on which moles feed.

Pine mice burrow underground and cut off plant roots. Watch for small exit holes and speedy run-off of water. Place poisoned food inside the holes, and cover with pieces of tile or boards to protect other animals.

Conquering Chlorosis

Chlorosis, an unnatural yellowing of rose foliage in which the veins usually stay darker green, is caused by an iron shortage that results from poor drainage, excess lime in the soil, naturally alkaline soils, or lack of organic matter. The best prevention is to prepare the planting site properly, based on results of a soil test (see page 20). Roses with some yellow or orange shadings in the petals are most susceptible to chlorosis. For mild cases, spray the leaves with liquid iron.

For severe cases, try one of the following remedies:

1. Improve soil conditions by mixing manure and agricultural sulfur into the surface soil. Use a ratio of 2 pounds sulfur to 1 cubic foot of manure.

2. Bore a tiny hole (about the size of a small finishing nail) into all canes that are 1/2 inch or larger in diameter. Fill the holes with iron citrate and seal with pruning paint.

3. Add soluble iron to the roots. Make 3- to 6-inch-deep holes in moist soil in the root area. Put about 1 ounce of ferrous (iron) sulfate in each hole and cover with soil. Apply 1/2 to 1 pound per bush, depending upon the plant's size. Each irrigation will diffuse enough soluble iron to the root system to supply the plant. Generally, a single treatment is effective for up to 4 years.

4. Apply one of the more expensive chelated irons. Follow the manufacturer's directions.

Aphids

Japanese beetles

Blackspot

Symptoms		Problems	Solutions
Clusters of tiny insects on young shoots, flower buds, or under-side of leaves. Foliage and blooms stunted or deformed. Sticky honeydew left behind attracts ants.	Enlarged 2x	APHIDS. Soft-bodied, green, brown, or reddish insects that suck plant juices.	Harmless lady beetles added to the garden will feed on aphids. Wipe out infestations with contact sprays such as Diazinon, Malathion, Sevin, Orthene.
Foliage, flowers, and stems are chewed, devoured, or have holes drilled in them.	All life size	BEETLES (including, 1. Japanese, 2. rose chafer, 3. rose curculio, and 4. Fuller beetles). Their larvae also eat plant roots.	Pick off beetles by hand or knock them into a can of kerosene and water. Spray with Sevin, Diazinon, or Malathion.
Circular black spots with fringed margins appear on leaves. Leaves may turn yellow and drop prematurely. On more resistant varieties, leaves will remain green and hang onto bush.		BLACKSPOT. A fungus disease, easily spread to nearby bushes by rain or hose. Overwinters in small cane lesions or leaves left on ground.	Water with wand or soil soaker. If you must wet foliage, do it from overhead and early in day, so bush can dry before night. Apply fungicides such as Phaltan and Captan.
Grayish-brown growth on buds and partially opened flowers, especially pink and white hybrid teas. The diseased flowers come apart easily when touched.		BOTRYTIS BLIGHT. A fungus disease that over-winters on infected plant parts.	Pick off and destroy faded and infected blooms. Spray with fungicides. Read labels for recommendations.
Flower buds eaten or leaves rolled and tied around the pest, eaten from inside. Most often a late spring problem.	Life size	BUDWORM AND OTHER CATERPILLARS. Larvae of moths and butterflies that feed on rose foliage.	Cut out infested buds and leaves. Apply Diazinon, Sevin, or Orthene.
Holes eaten into leaves from the underside, causing a skeleton-ized glazed effect. Appear early in the spring. Later, large holes eaten in leaves and, finally, the veins are devoured.	Approx. life size	BRISTLY ROSE SLUGS (Often called cane borers or leafworms.) Half-inch long, hairy, slimy larvae of sawfly; when young, eat underside of leaves, when mature, eat entire leaf.	Act quickly to stop their speedy damage. Spray with Sevin.
Lesions in the woody tissue of a cane, poor growth, or death above the affected area.		CANKER. A disease caused by parasitic fungus that usually enters plant through wounds or dying tissue.	Prune out and burn all affected areas, cutting well below canker with shears dipped in alcohol after each cut. Paint with pruning paint or spray. Same treatment as for black-spot will help.
Roundish, rough-surfaced growths near plant's crown or on roots. Plants lose vigor, produce abnormal flowers and foliage, and eventually die.		CROWN GALL. Soil-borne bacterial disease which can live on in soil after affected plant is removed and may or may not affect a new plant.	Do not buy plants with swell-ings near bud union or on roots. Remove and burn infected parts, seal with pruning paint. Or remove entire bush and treat soil with all-purpose fumigant before setting new plants.
Top surface of leaves turns pale and becomes covered with tiny yellow specks similar to damage of spider mites.	Life size / Enlarged 3x	LEAFHOPPERS. Tiny, greenish yellow, jumping insects found on underside of leaves. They suck out contents of leaf cells.	Apply Diazinon or Malathion.
Pale green foliage and stunted growth in spite of good garden-ing practices. Root examination reveals abnormal swelling, knotty enlargements with tiny white eggs inside, discolored lesions, or dead tissue.	Enlarged approx. 5x / Eggs	NEMATODES. Disease caused by tiny animal pests that invade the roots of the plant.	Check with your County Agent or Agricultural Experiment Station for help in diagnosis and control. All-purpose soil fumigants or nematocides are beneficial.

Symptoms		Problems	Solutions
Holes in cut ends of canes or punctures in stems. Wilting of plant shoot, foliage, and canes. Sometimes slight swelling of canes.		PITHBORERS (including, 1. rose stem sawfly, 2. rose stem girdler, and 3. small carpenter bees). Pests bore into cane and lay eggs. Larvae eat through canes.	Cut out canes below infested portion during spring pruning. Seal exposed tips with pruning paint.
White powdery masses of spores on young leaves, shoots, and buds; distorted young shoots; stunted foliage.		POWDERY MILDEW. Disease spread by wind. Encouraged by warm days followed by cool nights. Overwinters on fallen leaves and inside stems and bud scales.	Apply Parnon or Phaltan. For best results, apply when mildew is first noticed.
Large mossy or callus swellings on stems, or roots. Look like crown gall, but if cut open, you'll find larvae. (Mostly on species roses.)		ROSE GALL (including mossy rose gall, and rose root gall). Caused by wasplike insects that bore into canes and lay eggs. The growing larvae cause swelling.	Insecticides do not control. Prune infested stems and burn to destroy larvae before they emerge. Seal exposed area.
Black, deformed flower buds and leaves that die prematurely.	Enlarged 3x	ROSE MIDGE. Tiny, yellowish flies lay eggs in growing tips of stems. Hatching maggots destroy tender tissue.	Remove and destroy affected areas. Spray with Orthene.
Wilting and darkening of foliage, which drops prematurely. Close examination reveals mature stems encrusted with hard-shelled insects.	Approx. life size	ROSE SCALES. Round, dirty white, gray, or brown shell-covered insects that suck sap from plants.	Prune out and destroy old, infested wood. Apply Malathion, Sevin, Orthene, Dormant Oil Spray.
Wilted leaves that may drop. Yellow dots and light green mottling appear on upper leaf surface opposite pustules of powdery, rust-colored spores on the lower surface.		RUST. Overwinters in fallen leaves, spread by wind. The disease is especially troublesome along the Pacific Coast.	Remove and destroy all rusted leaves during pruning. Apply lime-sulfur spray as a dormant spray. Select rust-resistant varieties when planting new roses.
Stippled leaves appear dry, turn brown, red, yellow, or gray, then curl and drop off. Sometimes webs are visible on the underside of leaves.		SPIDER MITES. Minute pests that suck juices from underside of rose foliage. Abundant in hot, dry weather.	Clean up trash and weeds in early spring to destroy breeding places. Spray infestations with Diazinon, Orthene, Malathion, Dormant Oil Spray.
White spots with dark red rims, turning yellow. Leaves develop holes and fall off. There may be brown raised spots on stems.		SPOT ANTHRACNOSE. A fungus disease. Overwinters in infected stem, and spores are spread by spring rains.	Prune out infected canes in spring. Apply fungicide. Read labels for recommendations.
Flecked petals and deformed flowers, especially on white varieties.		THRIPS. Very active, tiny, slender, brownish-yellow, winged insects. Hide in base of infected flowers.	Cut off and dispose of spent blooms. Apply Diazinon, Malathion, Orthene.
Small, angular, colorless spots on foliage. Ring, oakleaf, water-mark, or mosaic patterns develop on leaves.		VIRUS DISEASES (including Mosaic). Spread by propagation of infected plants.	Prevention is only control. Do not buy any plants exhibiting the symptoms described. Dispose of entire affected plants to prevent spread of virus to other nearby plants.

Protection From The Elements

Any strong wind is bad for roses. Brisk ocean breezes can damage nearby plants. And the salt spray in the air isn't helpful, either. A hedge of protective shrubs or a fence helps shield roses from these abrasive conditions.

A hot dry wind spells trouble for roses. To protect them, plant a screen of shrubs or trees to slow the wind down and add some moisture to the wind as it passes through.

A fence might seem to be a plausible remedy, but it just won't do the job. Air on the leeward side of a fence is more turbulent than it is on the leeward side of a hedge. And, most importantly, a fence won't add moisture to dry air as a shrub will.

Allow at least 10 feet of distance between rose bushes and a screen or hedge. Select deep-rooted shrubs that do well in your climate. Ask your nurseryman how close to space them together so they will form a solid screen.

Hot weather fatigues a rose plant. At temperatures above 90°F., the plant uses food faster than its leaf factory can manufacture it. If you live in a hot climate, don't prune back roses as much as rosarians do in cooler environments. During the winter, prune only enough to shape the plants the way you want them. The plant needs to be big and leafy when spring comes to enable photosynthesis to build the plant up before summer heat arrives.

In extremely hot, sunny areas, you might consider adding a lath cover over at least a portion of the rose garden to give some shade during the hottest part of the day.

Cool nights or dark, damp days can cause "balling," or half-opened blooms. Cut off such blooms when they start to ball, so that better new growth can begin when weather conditions improve.

If you live in a cool or foggy area, select rose varieties with fewer petals to ensure opening.

Sudden temperature changes in the fall, before the plant has hardened off for winter, can be disastrous. Early freezes kill more canes than much colder freezes later on in winter do. In areas where early freezes are likely, avoid late-summer feedings and hold back on water.

Freezes in late winter or early spring kill shoots that have been forced during warm winter days. Don't prune your roses until all danger of frost is past.

Sometimes, after very mild or warm winters, branch tips may remain bare, or the side buds on some canes may fail to open. This occurs because they were not chilled enough to induce normal growth. Prune out such canes.

In extremely warm regions, prune in winter and remove all leaves from the plants by hand. This forces a period of dormancy.

Protect container roses from flooding during heavy rains by moving them to a sheltered area, or securing heavy-duty plastic covering around the stems and over the top of the pot.

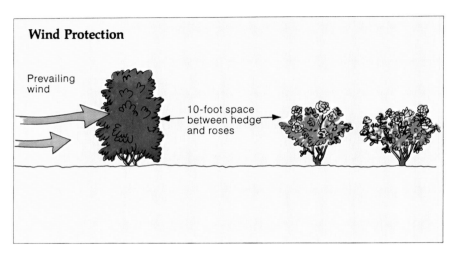

Wind Protection

Prevailing wind

10-foot space between hedge and roses

When you grow roses for exhibition, injury from wind or rain can ruin everything. Hot sunshine can fade the colors just before show time. To protect specimen blooms, cover them with light plastic bags clipped together at the bottom. Be sure to leave enough of an opening for air to pass through.

Or make a cone-shaped cap of plastic or heavy paper and attach it to stakes next to the plant to cover the bloom. Move the cap, as needed, with clips hooked to the stake. To delay a bud opening or to hold a color longer, use caps of black paper or dark plastic.

Pruning Bush Roses For Better Production

An unpruned rose can grow into a mass of tangled brambles that produces small or inferior blooms. Proper pruning removes unproductive or damaged wood and leaves a few good canes as the foundation of a healthy bush. Pruning gives the rose plant an attractive shape and keeps it a desired size for your landscape design. And good pruning practices improve flower quality, as well.

When To Prune?

Prune just before the rose bush breaks dormancy. The right time can be anytime between January in warm areas to April in very cold zones. Check with your County Extension Service for suggested local dates.

Don't prune roses until you have removed winter protection completely and the danger of frost is past. (Frost can make a second pruning necessary.) Prune before new leaves develop to prevent loss of sap from cut surfaces.

Use The Right Equipment

You'll need three types of cutting instruments. Make sure they have sharp blades and are well lubricated.

1. A fine-toothed, curved saw for cutting woody tissue.
2. Pruning shears with one cutting blade working against an anvil.
3. Long-handled lopping shears for thick canes or getting into hard-to-reach places.

In addition, you'll need a pair of heavy-duty leather garden gloves and pruning paint to seal major cuts.

Make Cuts Correctly

Cut at sharp 45°-65° angles. Do not leave any bare stubs that can contract diseases. Make all cuts down to a cane, to the point on the crown from which the cane originated, or to a strong outside bud, or "eye," on stem nodes. This eye is the origin of all new replacement growth. Make cuts about 1/4 inch above the bud.

When using pruning shears, make sure the cutting blade is on the lower side to ensure a clean cut. Put pressure on the noncutting side so that the injury will occur on the top part of the cane—the part that will be discarded.

How Much To Prune?

There are three basic types of pruning:

Severe or heavy. Cut the plant back to 3 or 4 canes, 6 to 10 inches high. This method produces showy blooms. Prune only vigorous, well-established bushes in this manner. Severe pruning of weak bushes sacrifices the plant's vigor and reduces the bush's lifespan.

Moderate. Leave 5 to 12 canes, about 18 to 24 inches high. Moderate pruning develops a much larger bush than severe pruning does, and is the best method for most garden roses.

Light. Cut at a minimum; plants should remain 3 to 4 feet in height. Light pruning produces a profusion of short-stemmed flowers on larger bushes. This method is practiced mainly with floribundas, grandifloras, first-year hybrid teas, species roses, and weak-growing varieties of all classes.

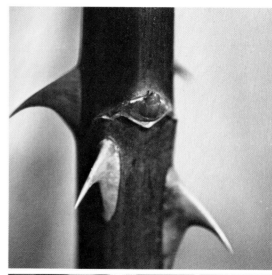

Top: All replacement growth comes from buds or "eyes" that are found on sides of cane at the base of leaf or just above the leaf scar. Look for single buds and make pruning cuts 1/4 inch above. Bottom: Eliminate any double buds during pruning to prevent undesirable double-headed cane growth.

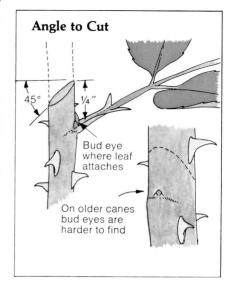

Angle to Cut

45°   1/4"

Bud eye where leaf attaches

On older canes bud eyes are harder to find

Bud union

Sucker

Within the same climatic zone, various rosarians will practice all three methods. Experience will show which method works best for you. It usually takes several years to learn the best method for each variety of rose you prune. Don't be shy when it comes to taking off growth. Most roses are hardy shrubs and will bounce back with plenty of new growth.

Pruning Procedure

You will find heavy pruning easier if the bud union is above ground. If you have planted below the soil level, you might want to remove soil from around the bud union during pruning so that you can see the origin of all the canes.

First, remove any dead wood down to the nearest healthy, dormant bud. Make the cut at least 1 inch below the dead area. If no live buds remain, remove the entire branch or cane to the bud union.

Examine carefully for canker or other diseased areas (see pages 42-43). Cut down to a good bud at least an inch below any evidence of disease. Although canes may look healthy, the pith may contain a problem. To find out, cut the top of each cane and check inside. The pith should be creamy white, not brown or gray. Prune down to where pith is healthy, or to the bud union if pith is diseased all the way through.

Cut out weak, spindly, or deformed growth, including canes that grow straight out and then curve upward (doglegs). Remove the canes that grow toward the center of the bush. If 2 branches cross, remove the weaker one.

Remove all suckers or reversion growth (undesired shoots that come from the rootstock below the bud union). If you do not remove suckers, they will soon dominate the plant. Sucker foliage differs in color and form from the rest of the plant. When cutting, take all of the sucker base from the crown area; you can even remove a piece of the crown, if necessary.

Next, thin out the remaining healthy canes to the desired shape, and cut them down to the selected height. After severe winters, you may have to cut all the canes to within several inches of the bud union. If so, you can't worry about shape; just save as much live wood as you can.

Seal all major cuts with pruning paint to aid in healing wounds and to keep out insects and diseases.

Moderate pruning produces larger plants,
the best method for landscape roses.

1. Unpruned hybrid tea rose. **2.** Cut out old or dead canes and branches. **3.** Remove canes with signs of disease. **4.** Remove canes to create desired shape. **5.** Cut back tops to selected height. **6.** Apply pruning paint to all major cuts.

Suckers grow from the rootstock below the bud union. They must be completely removed or they will soon dominate the plant. Dig down below the bud union to find the source of the sucker growth. Remove it down to its base, along with part of the crown, if necessary.

This rose bush has been pruned back severely to produce exhibition-quality roses.

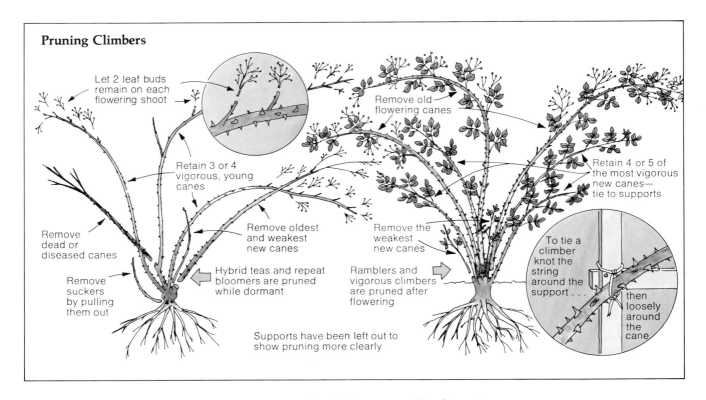

Pruning Climbers

Let 2 leaf buds remain on each flowering shoot

Retain 3 or 4 vigorous, young canes

Remove dead or diseased canes

Remove suckers by pulling them out

Hybrid teas and repeat bloomers are pruned while dormant

Remove oldest and weakest new canes

Remove old flowering canes

Remove the weakest new canes

Ramblers and vigorous climbers are pruned after flowering

Retain 4 or 5 of the most vigorous new canes—tie to supports

To tie a climber knot the string around the support . . .

then loosely around the cane

Supports have been left out to show pruning more clearly

Pruning And Training Climbing Roses

Prune ramblers and vigorous climbing roses soon after they have flowered. Cut out diseased canes, dead canes, older gray canes, and weak new canes. Most climber canes are good for only 2 or 3 seasons. Save the green healthy canes. Cut laterals back to 8 to 10 buds to shape the plant as desired. Be sure to remove any suckers.

Some of the less vigorous climbers need to be trimmed each spring only, to remove winterkill. Remove the faded flowers later, after blooming has stopped.

Prune hybrid climbers and everblooming large-flowered climbers while they're still dormant. Do not take as much wood from the everbloomers as from the hybrids. Proceed as you would with bush roses: remove dead and diseased canes; get rid of any sucker growth; and remove old growth or weak new growth. Retain 3 or 4 vigorous young canes.

Keep flowers plucked off everblooming roses as soon as possible after peak bloom. Do not take the foliage, however—reblooming occurs from the top leaves, immediately under the old flower cluster. When removing hybrid blooms, leave 2 leaf buds on each flowering shoot.

Prune all climbers to make them fit their training supports—arbors, fences, pergolas, pillars, or trellises. Train them by arching or tying them to a horizontal position; point their tips downward to make every bud produce a flowering branch. (See diagram for directions on how to tie them up.)

Shortening some of the long canes will stimulate the laterals to develop, continue to elongate, and cover the support.

1. Strip foliage to reveal growth pattern.
2. Remove old canes with loppers. **3.** Tie remaining canes to the support.

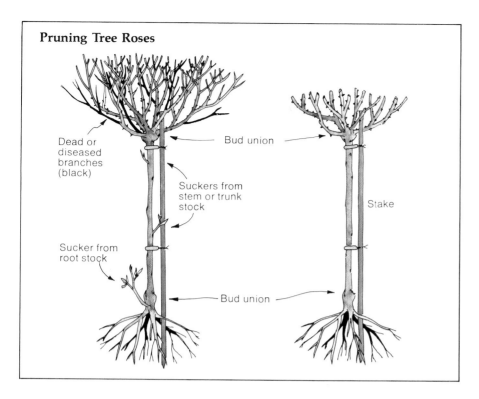

Pruning Tree Roses (within illustration)

Dead or diseased branches (black)

Bud union

Suckers from stem or trunk stock

Stake

Sucker from root stock

Bud union

Pruning Tree Roses

Prune standards just like bush roses: cut out dead or diseased branches or canes, and prune the healthy canes back to a good bud. Keep the shape as symmetrical as possible so the foliage will fill out into a full, round shape.

Suckers are twice as likely to occur on tree roses as on bush plants. They can grow from the rootstock or from the trunkstock. Cut them out as close to their base as possible.

Pruning Old-Fashioned, Shrub, Or Species Roses

There are many roses that fit into this category, and almost as many ways to prune and train. Your best bet is to consult the nursery that sold you the plant, or to read a few of the books devoted to growing these roses.

Basically, there are two methods of pruning, for two types of bloomers:

Annual bloomers should not be pruned until after they have bloomed. At that point, shorten the long canes by 1/3 and the lateral canes a few inches.

Repeat bloomers should be trimmed to a good shape, not cut back. Keep faded flowers plucked during blooming to encourage new flowering stems.

Don't Put Away The Pruning Shears

Keep pruning and grooming roses as they grow. Throughout the season, continue to cut out weak and spindly shoots, suckers, and obvious signs of disease. Remove old flowers as soon as they have passed their peak.

Flowers of hybrid teas are produced in waves. Allowing the plant to set seeds increases the interval between periods of bloom. In removing fading flowers, don't just snip off the flower; cut back to a 5-leaflet leaf. Cuts at these major leaves result in stronger foliage breaks as the plant continues to develop. During the first growing season of a newly planted rose, snip only the flowers; a young plant needs all the leaves it can produce. In cold-winter areas, allow the seed pods (hips) to form on the final wave of bloom. The formation of hips slows down growth and hardens the plant for winter.

Rosarians who want to produce large, exhibition-quality blooms disbud most of the side vegetative buds and flowers and allow only one or a selected few terminal buds to mature.

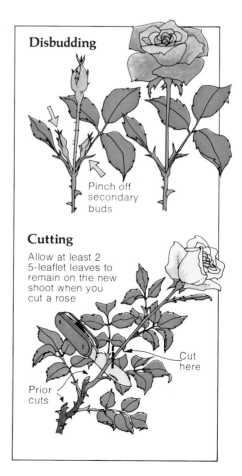

Disbudding

Pinch off secondary buds

Cutting

Allow at least 2 5-leaflet leaves to remain on the new shoot when you cut a rose

Cut here

Prior cuts

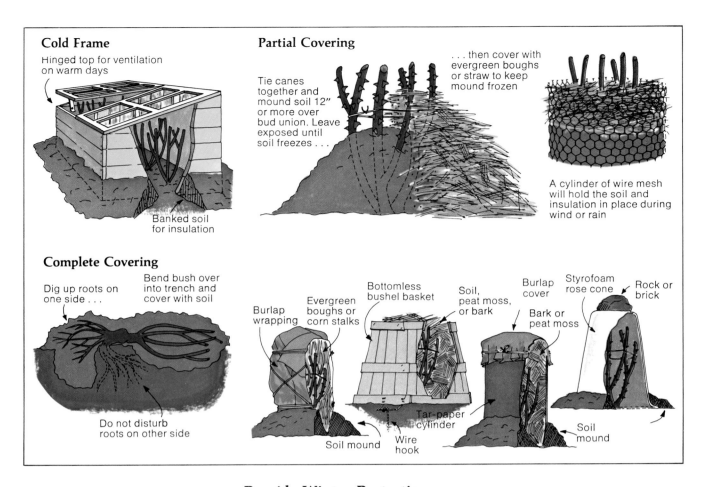

Cold Frame

Hinged top for ventilation on warm days

Banked soil for insulation

Partial Covering

Tie canes together and mound soil 12" or more over bud union. Leave exposed until soil freezes . . .

. . . then cover with evergreen boughs or straw to keep mound frozen

A cylinder of wire mesh will hold the soil and insulation in place during wind or rain

Complete Covering

Dig up roots on one side . . .

Bend bush over into trench and cover with soil

Do not disturb roots on other side

Burlap wrapping

Evergreen boughs or corn stalks

Bottomless bushel basket

Soil, peat moss, or bark

Burlap cover

Bark or peat moss

Styrofoam rose cone

Rock or brick

Tar-paper cylinder

Soil mound

Wire hook

Soil mound

Soil mound

Provide Winter Protection

This is probably the most controversial area of rose culture. Some experts go so far as to advise against any winter protection except mulch, even in pretty cold climates. Other people in the same area recommend tipping and burying the entire plant. Once again, we suggest calling upon your County Extension Agent for help in determining what kind of protection most suits your own locality and your own style of gardening.

Many roses, including quite a few species, shrubs, and climbers, are naturally cold-hardy and need little or no protection. A number of newer hybrid teas, marketed as subzero plants, are reported to need little protection. We talked to rosarians who said, however, that these "subzero" plants need just as much covering as other hybrids do.

One of the best ways of protecting a plant against cold-weather damage is by giving proper summer care. Vigorous bushes can withstand cold far better than unhealthy ones can. Roses planted in locations that are sheltered by trees, large shrubs, or structures need less protection than bushes that are exposed to the elements.

Where temperatures drop to 10° to 15° F. for as much as 2 weeks at a time, you can protect most bush roses adequately by mounding the base of each plant with fresh, loose soil or well-draining compost. Immediately after the first frost, mound up soil 6 to 8 inches high. Some growers advise cutting back plants to as much as 16 to 30 inches before mounding. If you do this, be sure to clean up and dispose of all clippings to cut down disease spread. In any case, apply a final coat of dormant spray before mounding. Now you can tie the canes together to protect them from winds, if you like.

Add hay or straw over the mound and exposed canes after the first hard freeze to protect against fluctuating temperatures and the freezing and thawing of soil around the canes.

Rose caps are available from horticultural houses, or you can devise your own cover. If you use caps, prune the plant first, so it fits underneath.

If you live in an area where salt is used on roads, protect your plants by spreading plastic over the soil after the first hard freeze, then covering the plastic with straw or hay.

Where temperatures dip below zero, you may need additional protection. We've illustrated ideas from quite a few rosarians.

Exercise care when you remove winter coverings in the spring. Don't get too anxious to unwrap them—even a light freeze can kill the tender growth underneath. Keep some straw or mulch material handy to cover the plants, in the event of a late frost.

Tree Roses

In mild-winter areas, wrap the plants in straw and cover with burlap. In temperate zones, no protection is necessary.

If the temperature goes as low as 10° F., in late fall dig under the roots on one side, until you can pull the plant over on the ground without breaking the root connections with the soil. Stake the plant to the ground and cover the entire plant with several inches of soil.

In spring, after the soil has thawed and the frost danger is past, remove the soil and set the plant upright once again.

Climbing Roses

A burlap wrapping is adequate protection in mild-winter climates. But in areas with hard freezes, you can bury climbers as you would tree roses.

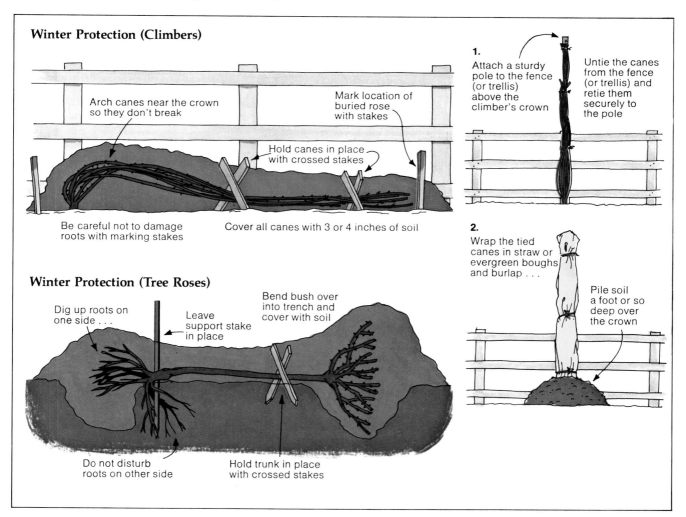

Winter Protection (Climbers)

Arch canes near the crown so they don't break

Mark location of buried rose with stakes

Hold canes in place with crossed stakes

Be careful not to damage roots with marking stakes

Cover all canes with 3 or 4 inches of soil

1.
Attach a sturdy pole to the fence (or trellis) above the climber's crown

Untie the canes from the fence (or trellis) and retie them securely to the pole

2.
Wrap the tied canes in straw or evergreen boughs and burlap . . .

Pile soil a foot or so deep over the crown

Winter Protection (Tree Roses)

Dig up roots on one side . . .

Leave support stake in place

Bend bush over into trench and cover with soil

Do not disturb roots on other side

Hold trunk in place with crossed stakes

Different forms of roses need different types of pruning. Climbers especially benefit from an occasional pruning—see page 48 for specifics.

Reviving Old Neglected Roses

Contrary to popular belief, roses are very tough. On farms that have been abandoned for 50 years, sometimes the only plants found still growing will be asparagus and roses. The roses will probably be old varieties, rambler or shrub, but many of the newer hybrid tea roses also sink tap roots deep enough to last many years.

What is the first step in pruning an old, neglected rose? Remove all broken, dead and diseased parts; then prune away all weak, twiggy and inward-growing wood, and wood that is rubbing against another branch.

Open up the center of the bush by pruning to vigorous outward-facing buds. Cut back young wood to 2 to 3 buds. Fertilize and spray for fungus and insects. That's about all you should do the first year; to do more might send the plant into shock.

During the following dormant period, cut out an old branch at ground level. Reduce one of the remaining old branches by half and cut back two-thirds— not just one-third—of the new wood. Repeat this the next winter and the third winter as well, if necessary. You should end up with a rose bush that has no wood over three years old. Each year during revival pruning, you should see an increase in new wood and better quality roses. If not, you'd better dig up the old rose and replace it with a promising new one.

Below: Formal gardens rely on more or less constant surveillance with pruning shears in hand. Right: An arbor of roughly cut timbers covered with an informal climbing rose at Old Westbury Gardens in Long Island, New York—the essence of natural beauty.

Described as a pink blend, the floribunda
Vogue was introduced in 1952 and was
an All-America Selection.

ENCYCLOPEDIA OF ROSES

*Want to know the particulars on
a specific rose? Use the charts
on the following pages as a quick
reference—or take it to the nursery
with you when you purchase
dormant bare-root roses.*

The following pages list the roses obtainable from commercial sources in the United States and Canada. This is intended only as a guide—by no means is it a complete listing of what's available. However, it does represent some of the most popular, easy-to-grow varieties, and a few forgotten or very new cultivars that deserve your attention.

Roses are divided by classification so that you can find them according to their basic growth habits. All spelling and information are based on listings of the American Rose Society. If you have a particular rose in mind that you want to find in the chart but don't know whether it's a hybrid tea, a floribunda, or a grandiflora, look for the variety name in the index in the back of the book first.

Column one of the chart gives the name of the rose cultivar or species, along with the year of its commercial introduction.

Column two gives the bloom color. Under flower description, you can locate the size, form (single, semidouble, or double), number of petals (to determine fullness), and fragrance. Next follows a brief description of the foliage and the growth habits of the plant.

The final column lists sources that offered the plant for sale at the time of publication. The numbers correspond to the catalog list on page 140. Suppliers change their stock regularly, so you may have to contact more than one source to find a particular rose you want.

Most catalogs are sent free of charge, but some cost a nominal amount, refundable with your first order. We advise sending away for as many catalogs as possible. Not only do they make for great garden daydreaming during those gray winter days, but they are also very educational. Many catalogs contain quality information on varieties, cultures, history, and helpful tips. Just reading through them will make you more knowledgeable about variety characteristics. Catalog writers are a unique lot, and each catalog usually has its own personality. Whether or not you order from the catalogs you read, don't miss out on this valuable source of gardening information.

Select Roses That Are Best For You

Learn to make competent decisions about the rose varieties you want to grow. Consider the type of blooms you want and the requirements of your landscape. Check gardens in the neighborhood, and observe which roses perform best. Contact local garden clubs and rose societies for suggestions about varieties suitable to your area. Visit public rose gardens and look at the wide-ranging display of roses. Spend a few winter hours poring over rose descriptions in mail-order catalogs. (See list on page 140.)

Consult our charts on the following pages for descriptions of readily available commercial roses. Call your County Agent or write the State Cooperative Extension Service for published lists of variety recommendations that grow well in your state. See pages 138-139 for addresses of the various State Cooperative Extension Services.

Bewitched

Candy Stripe

Apollo

Antigua

Hybrid Teas

Rose and year of introduction	Color	Flower description	Foliage and growth habits	Catalog sources
American Heritage (1965) †	Ivory and salmon	3-5" Double (50-60 petals), no fragrance	Dark, leathery; tall, compact, moderate blooming	9, 77, 80, 92
American Pride (1979)	Deep red	4½-5½" Double flowers open from oval-shaped buds. Blooms freely; fragrant	Glossy green foliage; plant is extremely disease-resistant and vigorous	8, 92
Antigua (1974)	Apricot blend	4½-6" Double (25-30 petals), heavy, fruity-spicy fragrance	Bronzy, glossy, leathery; medium green; disease-resistant	8, 77, 82, 92
Apollo (1971) †	Medium yellow	5-6" Double (30-35 petals), moderate to strong fragrance	Dark, glossy, leathery; disease-resistant, few thorns	55, 65, 77, 80, 84, 86, 92
Arctic Flame (1955)	Bright red	5" Double (50-60 petals), moderate fragrance	Medium green; subzero plant, very vigorous	9, 12, 77
Beauté (1953)	Light orange	Large double, moderate fragrance	Vigorous, free-blooming	70, 77, 80, 92
Bewitched (1967) †	Rose Bengal	5" Double (24-30 petals), spicy, old-fashioned fragrance	Glossy; easy to grow	55, 77, 80, 86, 89, 92
Big Ben (1964)	Dark red	5-6" Double, heavy fragrance	Dark; tall-growing	12, 61, 70, 77, 80, 86, 92
Blanche Mallerin (1941)	Pure white	4" Double (30-35 petals), moderate fragrance	Glossy, leathery; vigorous, few thorns	55, 86, 92
Blue Moon (1964)	Lilac	4" Double (40 petals), heavy fragrance	Medium green; very vigorous, free-blooming	61, 77, 92
Candy Stripe (1963)	Dusty pink streaked lighter	6" Double (60 petals), heavy, tea-rose fragrance	Dark, glossy; well-shaped plant	58, 77, 86
Carla (1963)	Pink shaded salmon	3½-5" Double (26 petals), moderate fragrance	Dark; vigorous, free-blooming	58, 61, 92
Charlotte Armstrong (1940) †	Red to cerise	3-4" Double (35 petals), moderate tea-rose fragrance	Dark, leathery; very vigorous, compact, abundant bloom	8, 9, 10, 22, 55, 58, 63, 69, 80, 86, 88
Chicago Peace (1962)	Pink and yellow	5-5½" Double (50-60 petals), slight fragrance, good exhibition rose	Glossy, leathery; vigorous, upright, bushy	5, 22, 55, 61, 65, 69, 80, 84, 86, 87, 89, 92

† All-America Rose Selection

Chrysler Imperial

Command Performance

Double Delight

Electron

Rose and year of introduction	Color	Flower description	Foliage and growth habits	Catalog sources
Christian Dior (1958) †	Crimson flushed scarlet	4-4½" Double (50-60 petals), slight fragrance	Dark, glossy, leathery; bushy plant, abundant blooms	69, 77, 86, 87, 92
Chrysler Imperial (1952) †	Crimson-red	4½-5" Double (40-50 petals), heavy fragrance	Dark; moderate-blooming	5, 9, 10, 12, 18, 22, 55, 58, 61, 63, 65, 77, 80, 86, 87, 89, 92
Color Magic †	Ivory pink to clear coral	6-7" Double (25-30 petals), light fragrance	Medium green foliage, on a vigorous growing plant	4, 8, 9, 10, 22, 55, 58, 62, 65, 80, 86, 87, 89, 92
Command Performance † (1970)	Orange-red	3-4" Semidouble (15-20 petals), heavy fragrance	Leathery; upright growth	58, 61, 65, 77, 80, 92
Confidence (1951)	Light pink to yellow	Large double (28-38 petals), moderate fragrance	Dark, leathery; vigorous and bushy	61, 87, 89, 92
Crimson Glory (1935)	Deep crimson with purple	Large double (30 petals), heavy, old-fashioned fragrance	Leathery; spreading	5, 9, 18, 22, 55, 58, 61, 63, 65, 77, 80, 86, 89, 90, 92
Dainty Bess (1925)	Rose-pink	3-4" Single (5 petals), moderate fragrance, good exhibition flower	Leathery; hardy plant	58, 61, 80, 86, 90, 92
Double Delight (1977) †	Red and white	5½-6" Double (35-45 petals), heavy, spicy fragrance	Dark, glossy; spreading, quite bushy plant	5, 8, 10, 18, 22, 58, 61, 62, 63, 65, 69, 80, 81, 86, 87, 89, 92
Eclipse (1935)	Golden yellow	3-5" Double (25-30 petals), moderate fragrance	Leathery; tall, shapely plant	26, 55, 58, 63, 65, 69, 80, 86, 87, 89, 92
Electron (1972) †	Rose-pink	Large double, slight fragrance	Glossy, light green; some disease-resistance, free-blooming, many thorns	55, 58, 61, 77, 80, 86, 92
Etoile de Hollande (1919)	Bright red	Large double (35-45 petals), heavy, old-fashioned fragrance	Medium green; moderate open growth	22, 80, 86
Firelight (1971)	Coral	6" Double, moderate fragrance	Leathery, light green; very vigorous, disease-resistant	77, 92
First Love (1951)	Rose to pink	2½-3½" Double (20-30 petals), slight fragrance	Leathery, light green; moderately bushy plant	61, 77, 86, 90
First Prize (1970) †	Rose-pink with ivory	6" Double (25 petals), moderate fragrance, top U.S. exhibition rose	Dark, leathery; disease-resistant, upright, angular	5, 8, 10, 22, 55, 58, 61, 65, 77, 80, 86, 87, 89, 92

† All-America Rose Selection

Flaming Peace

Helen Traubel

Gypsy

Heirloom

Hybrid Teas

Rose and year of introduction	Color	Flower description	Foliage and growth habits	Catalog sources
Flaming Peace (1965)	Crimson and yellow	Large double, moderate fragrance	Dark, glossy, leathery; abundant bloom	18, 61, 65, 69, 77, 80, 84, 92
Forty-Niner (1949) †	Cherry-red and yellow	3½-4″ Double (25-40 petals), slight fragrance	Dark, glossy, leathery; compact, free-blooming	12, 55, 65, 80, 87
Fragrant Cloud (1968)	Coral-red	5″ Double (25-30 petals), heavy, tea-rose fragrance, good show rose	Dark, glossy; very vigorous, very free-blooming	8, 55, 58, 61, 77, 80, 89, 90, 92
Fred Edmunds (1943) †	Coppery orange	5-5½″ Double (20-30 petals), heavy, spicy fragrance	Glossy, leathery; bushy, open	86, 87, 89
Friendship (1979) †	Glowing pink	5½-6″ Double (30-40 petals), sweet fragrance	Glossy foliage; upright growing, vigorous and extremely disease-resistant	5, 8, 10, 18, 55, 58, 62, 63, 65, 69, 80, 86, 87, 89
Garden Party (1959) †	Pale yellow to white	4-5″ Double (25-30 petals), slight fragrance, often tinted light pink	Semiglossy; vigorous, bushy, well-branched	10, 12, 61, 65, 69, 77, 83, 84, 86, 87, 89
Golden Masterpiece (1954)	Golden yellow	Very large double (35 petals), moderate fragrance	Glossy; vigorous, upright	12, 18, 22, 55, 77, 80, 92
Granada (1963) †	Rose, red, and yellow	4-5″ Double (18-25 petals), moderate fragrance	Leathery, crinkled; vigorous, upright	55, 58, 61, 77, 80, 86, 89
Gypsy (1972) †	Orange-red	5″ Double (35-40 petals), slight, spicy fragrance	Glossy, leathery; above-average height	22, 58, 65, 77, 80, 86, 87, 92
Heirloom (1972)	Deep lilac	4½″ Double (35 petals), heavy fragrance	Dark, leathery; disease-resistant, profuse blooming	77, 80
Helen Traubel (1951) †	Pink to apricot	5-6″ Double (20-25 petals), moderate fragrance, weak neck	Leathery, olive-green; tall, vigorous	8, 22, 55, 58, 61, 62, 69, 77, 80, 86, 87, 89, 92
Honor (1980) †	Pure white	4-5″ Double, classic form	Leathery, olive-green; vigorous and upright growing	8, 9, 18, 55, 58
Irish Gold (1966)	Yellow	7″ Double (33 petals), moderate fragrance	Dark, glossy, leathery; upright, bushy plant	58, 61, 80, 92
John F. Kennedy (1965)	White	5-6″ Double (45-50 petals), heavy fragrance, long-lasting	Leathery; very vigorous, profuse bloom	5, 8, 10, 18, 55, 69, 77, 80, 86, 87, 89, 92
Kaiserin Auguste Viktoria (1891)	Snowy white tinted lemon	Large double (100 petals), heavy fragrance	Dark; intermittent bloom	22, 55, 69, 77, 89, 92

† All-America Rose Selection

Garden Party

Miss All-American Beauty

Medallion

Rose and year of introduction	Color	Flower description	Foliage and growth habits	Catalog sources
Katherine T. Marshall (1943) †	Rose-pink flushed yellow	5" Double (22 petals), light, spicy fragrance	Leathery; very vigorous, upright	26, 69
King's Ransom (1961) †	Golden yellow	5-6" Double (35-40 petals), moderate fragrance	Glossy, leathery; extremely long stems, not hardy	8, 18, 55, 58, 61, 65, 77, 86, 87, 89, 92
Kordes' Perfecta (1957)	Cream, crimson, and yellow	4½-5" Double (65-70 petals), heavy, tea-rose fragrance, hot climate intensifies color	Dark, glossy, leathery	5, 12, 18, 58, 61, 62, 69, 77, 80, 92
Lady X (1966)	Mauve	Large double, slight fragrance	Leathery; vigorous, upright growth	8, 12, 58, 61, 77, 86, 92
Lowell Thomas †	Golden yellow	4½-5" Double (35 petals), moderate fragrance	Dark green foliage, vigorous growing with good disease resistance	9, 10, 12, 65, 80, 86, 87, 92
Medallion (1973) †	Apricot-buff	7-8" Double (35 petals), moderate, fruity fragrance, good lasting quality	Leathery, light green; few thorns	8, 26, 55, 58, 61, 62, 65, 77, 80, 82, 86, 87, 89, 92
Mirandy (1945) †	Garnet-red	5-6" Double (40-50 petals), heavy, old-fashioned fragrance	Leathery; bushy, compact	5, 22, 55, 58, 62, 63, 65, 69, 77, 84, 87, 89, 92
Miss All-American † Beauty (1965)	Dark pink	4-5" Double (50-60 petals), heavy tea-rose fragrance, long-lasting blooms	Leathery; disease-resistant	55, 58, 61, 65, 69, 77, 80, 87, 89, 92
Mister Lincoln (1964) †	Dark red	4½-6" Double (30-40 petals), heavy fragrance	Dark, leathery; moderate to free-blooming	5, 18, 55, 58, 61, 62, 63, 65, 77, 80, 84, 86, 89, 92
Mojave (1954) †	Apricot-orange, tinted red	4-4½" Double (25 petals), prominently veined, moderate fragrance	Glossy, vigorous, upright	12, 18, 55, 58, 61, 62, 63, 65, 69, 77, 80, 86, 92
New Day (1972)	Soft yellow	4-4½" Double, good lasting quality and fragrance	Dark green, leathery foliage; thorny upright grower with excellent disease resistance	8, 86
Oklahoma (1964)	Very dark red	4-5½" Double (40-55 petals), heavy tea-rose fragrance	Dark, leathery; well-branched bushes	10, 55, 58, 77, 89, 92
Oregold (1975) †	Deep yellow	5" Double (35-40 petals), slight fragrance, color does not fade	Dark, glossy; disease-resistant, vigorous, upright, bushy	5, 8, 10, 22, 26, 55, 58, 61, 62, 63, 65, 77, 80, 82, 86, 87, 89, 92

† All-America Rose Selection

Pascali

Perfume Delight

Portrait

Hybrid Teas

Rose and year of introduction	Color	Flower description	Foliage and growth habits	Catalog sources
Papa Meilland (1963)	Dark crimson	Large double (35 petals), heavy fragrance	Glossy, leathery, olive-green; vigorous, upright growth	60, 61, 77, 92, 93
Paradise (1978) †	Lavender, trimmed magenta	5" Double (25-30 petals), long lasting with light fragrance	Dark, glossy; upright with good disease resistance	5, 8, 10, 18, 55, 58, 62, 63, 65, 69, 80, 86, 87, 89, 92
Pascali (1963) †	Creamy white	3-4" Double (30 petals), slight fragrance, good exhibition rose	Dark; vigorous, bushy, very free-blooming	55, 58, 61, 77, 80, 84, 86, 87, 92
Peace (1945) †	Yellow with rose-pink	6" Double (40-45 petals), slight fragrance, voted world's favorite rose	Very dark, glossy, leathery; very vigorous, tall, bushy	5, 8, 9, 10, 12, 18, 22, 26, 55, 58, 61, 62, 63, 65, 69, 77, 81, 82, 84, 86, 89, 92
Perfume Delight (1973) †	Pink	Large double, heavy, spicy fragrance	Leathery; abundant, continuous bloom, upright, bushy	5, 26, 55, 58, 61, 69, 77, 80, 82, 86, 87, 89, 92
Pink Peace (1959)	Deep pink	4½-6" Double (50-60 petals), heavy fragrance	Leathery; tall-growing, well-branched	9, 18, 55, 58, 63, 65, 69, 77, 80, 87, 89, 92
Portrait (1971) †	Pink	4" Double (35 petals), moderate fragrance, long-lasting	Dark, glossy, leathery; disease-resistant	77, 82, 92
Pristine (1977)	Ivory blushed pink	4½-6" Double (30-35 petals), with light fragrance	Dark, glossy, leathery; disease-resistant	8, 86, 92
Promise (1976)	Light pink	5-6" Double (35-45 petals), slight fragrance	Glossy, medium green; abundant bloom	8, 80
Proud Land (1969)	Deep red	4½-5½" Double (60 petals), moderate fragrance	Dark, leathery; very vigorous, upright growth	8, 77, 80, 82, 92
Queen o' the Lakes (1949)	Blood-red to carmine	Large double, moderate fragrance	Glossy; subzero plant, vigorous, bushy	9, 18, 77
Red Devil (1970)	Light red	Large double (72 petals), moderate fragrance	Glossy, medium green; very vigorous	77, 80, 82, 86, 92
Red Masterpiece (1974)	Dark red	6" Double (35-40 petals), heavy fragrance	Dark, leathery; mildews, profuse blooming	8, 77, 80, 92
Red Radiance (1916)	Crimson	Medium double (23 petals), heavy, old-fashioned fragrance	Leathery; very vigorous, abundant bloom	22, 87, 89
Royal Highness (1962) †	Light pink	5-5½" Double (40-50 petals), heavy, tea-rose fragrance	Dark, glossy, leathery; upright, well-shaped plants	55, 58, 65, 77, 80, 84, 86, 88, 92
Rubaiyat (1946) †	Rose-red	4½-5" Double (25 petals), heavy fragrance	Dark, leathery; quite hardy	65, 69, 77, 80, 92
Seashell (1976) †	Peach-pink	4-5" Double (35-40 petals), heavy fragrance	Dark; abundant bloom on very ornamental bush	5, 8, 22, 55, 58, 61, 62, 65, 80, 86, 87, 89

† All-America Rose Selection

Seashell

Smoky

Tropicana

Rose and year of introduction	Color	Flower description	Foliage and growth habits	Catalog sources
Smoky (1968)	Plum to orange-red	3½-4″ Double (30-35 petals), slight fragrance unusual ever-changing color	Light green; vigorous, upright	8, 80
Snowfire (1973)	Scarlet and white	4-5″ Double, slight fragrance	Dark, glossy; disease-resistant, many thorns	8, 77, 80, 86, 89, 92
South Seas (1962)	Coral-pink	6-7″ Double (45-50 petals), moderate fragrance	Leathery; vigorous, upright, prolific	77, 86, 87, 92
Sterling Silver (1957)	Lilac	3½″ Double (30 petals), heavy fragrance, open petals are grey in sunlight	Dark, glossy; vigorous, upright	5, 8, 9, 18, 26, 55, 58, 62, 65, 80, 86, 89
Summer Sunshine (1962)	Deep yellow	3½-5″ Double (25 petals), slight fragrance	Dark, leathery; well-branched, abundant bloom	55, 69, 77, 80, 86, 87, 89, 92
Sunset Jubilee (1973)	Medium pink	6″ Double (40 petals), slight fragrance	Leathery, light green; abundant, continuous bloom	77, 80, 86, 92
Sutter's Gold (1950) [†]	Golden orange	4-5″ Double (30-35 petals), heavy fragrance	Dark, leathery; very vigorous	5, 22, 55, 58, 63, 65, 77, 80, 86, 89, 92
Swarthmore (1963)	Rose-red	4″ Double (45-55 petals), slight fragrance	Dark, leathery; very vigorous, bushy	58, 61, 62, 77, 89, 92
Talisman (1929)	Yellow and copper	Medium double (25 petals), moderate fragrance, an old favorite bicolor	Glossy, leathery, light green; vigorous	5, 22, 26, 55, 62, 69, 80, 86, 87, 89
The Doctor (1936)	Satiny pink	6″ Double (25 petals), heavy fragrance, huge flowers worth waiting for	Light green; dwarf, bushy	5, 9, 12, 65, 80, 87, 90
Tiffany (1954) [†]	Rose to pink	4-5″ Double (25-30 petals), heavy fragrance	Dark; very vigorous, upright	22, 55, 58, 61, 62, 65, 69, 77, 80, 81, 86, 87, 89, 92
Tropicana (1960) [†]	Coral-orange	5″ Double (30-35 petals), heavy, fruity fragrance, colorfast	Dark, glossy, leathery; exceptionally vigorous	5, 8, 9, 10, 12, 22, 55, 61, 62, 63, 65, 69, 70, 77, 80, 84, 86, 89, 92
V For Victory (1941)	Yellow tinted orange	Large Double (45 petals), heavy fragrance	Glossy; subzero plant, bushy	9, 10, 12, 18, 77
Whisky Mac (1967)	Bronze-yellow	Large Double (28-30 petals), heavy fragrance	Glossy; very vigorous and bushy	12, 61, 77, 80, 92
White Masterpiece (1969)	White	6″ Double (60 petals), slight fragrance	Glossy; compact plant	8, 61, 77, 80, 86, 92
Yankee Doodle (1976) [†]	Peach to apricot-yellow	5″ Double (50 petals), slight, tea-rose fragrance	Dark, glossy; outstanding disease-resistance	22, 26, 55, 58, 61, 62, 65, 69, 86, 87, 89

[†] All-America Rose Selection

Garnette

Cathedral

Redgold

Floribundas & Polyanthas

Rose and year of introduction	Color	Flower description	Foliage and growth habits	Catalog sources
Angel Face (1968) †	Lavender edged red	4″ Double (30-40 petals), heavy, old-fashioned fragrance, good exhibition rose	Dark, leathery; vigorous, upright, bushy	8, 10, 18, 22, 55, 58, 61, 62, 65, 77, 80, 87, 89, 92
Apricot Nectar (1965) †	Pink-apricot, golden base	4-4½″ Double (35-40 petals), fruity fragrance	Dark, glossy; good in hot areas, very disease-resistant	8, 61, 80, 92
Bahia (1974) †	Orange	4″ Double (20-30 petals), spicy fragrance	Bronzy, glossy; vigorous, hardy	55, 58, 61, 77, 92
Betty Prior (1935)	Carmine-pink	2-3″ Single (5 petals), moderate fragrance	Dark; hardy, disease-resistant	8, 55, 58, 63, 65, 69, 80, 87, 92
Cathedral (1976) †	Apricot to salmon	3-3½″ Double (15 petals), heavy fragrance	Glossy, olive-green; highly mildew-resistant	55, 58, 61, 62, 80
Cécile Brunner (1881)*	Bright pink/yellow	1-1½″ Double, moderate fragrance, the "sweetheart" rose	Dark; slow-growing	55, 80, 89, 92
Charisma (1977) †	Flame red/gold	2″ Double (35-40 petals), non-fading and long-lasting; mild fragrance	Olive green; vigorous, hardy and disease-resistant	8, 18, 55, 58, 62, 63, 65, 80, 87, 89
China Doll (1946)*	Rose-pink/yellow	1-2″ Double (20-26 petals), slight fragrance	Leathery; extremely profuse	55, 58, 69, 77, 87, 89
Circus (1956) †	Yellow pink-salmon, and scarlet	2½-3″ Double (45-58 petals), spicy tea fragrance	Leathery, semiglossy; compact and bushy	8, 26, 55, 65, 77, 80, 87
Europeana (1963) †	Dark crimson	3″ Double (25-30 petals), slight fragrance, top-rated exhibition floribunda	Bronze-green; very free-blooming	10, 18, 55, 58, 61, 62, 65, 77, 80, 87, 89, 92
Eutin (1940)	Carmine-red	2-3″ Double, slight fragrance	Dark, glossy, leathery; robust, disease-resistant	9, 10, 12, 18, 62, 65, 69, 77, 80, 89
Fashion (1949) †	Deep peach	3-3½″ Double (21-25 petals), moderate fragrance	Bronzy; disease-resistant spreading	9, 18, 58, 62, 65, 66, 69, 77, 80, 84, 87, 89, 92
First Edition (1977) †	Coral	2½″ Double, slight fragrance, color deepens in cool climate	Glossy, light green	10, 18, 58, 61, 62, 65, 87, 89, 92
Frensham (1946)	Deep scarlet	2-3″ Semidouble (15 petals), slight fragrance	Glossy; abundant, very free-blooming	61, 63, 65, 80, 90, 92

† All-America Rose Selection

The Fairy

Orangeade

Rose and year of introduction	Color	Flower description	Foliage and growth habits	Catalog sources
Garnette (1951)	Garnet-red/yellow	1-2″ Double (50 petals), slight fragrance, long-lasting flowers	Dark, leathery; susceptible to mildew	9, 80, 89, 90
Gene Boerner (1968) †	Deep pink	3½″ Double (35 petals), slight fragrance	Glossy; vigorous, upright	10, 55, 58, 61, 65, 77, 80, 92
Gold Cup †	Yellow	3″ Double	Glossy foliage on 2½′ plant	9, 18, 69, 92
Iceberg (1958)	White	2½-4″ Double, heavy fragrance	Glossy, light green; very disease-resistant	10, 55, 58, 61, 65, 69, 77, 79, 80, 86, 90, 92
Ivory Fashion (1958) †	Ivory white	4-4½″ Semidouble (15-18 petals), moderate fragrance	Leathery; vigorous, upright	58, 61, 69, 77, 90, 92
Little Darling (1956)	Yellow to salmon-pink	2½″ Double (24-30 petals), spicy fragrance	Dark, glossy, leathery; very vigorous	61, 77, 80, 92
Margo Koster (1931)*	Salmon	1-2″ Double, slight fragrance, clusters	Glossy; often sold as florist pot plant	55, 69, 80, 87, 89
Orangeade (1959)	Bright orange	2½″ Semidouble (7 petals), slight fragrance, long-lasting	Dark; vigorous, bushy	55, 61, 77, 92
Picnic (1976)	Coral-orange	4″ Double (25 petals), slight fragrance	Glossy; exceedingly free-blooming	8
Redgold (1971) †	Gold edged pink	2-3″ Double (25-30 petals), slight fragrance, very long-lasting	Light green	8, 9, 55, 58, 61, 62, 63, 65, 66, 77, 80, 89, 92
Red Pinocchio (1947)	Carmine-red	3″ Double (25-30 petals), moderate fragrance	Dark, leathery; tall and spreading in warmer climates	9, 62, 63, 65, 66, 77, 87, 89
Rose Parade (1975) †	Coral-pink	2½″ Double (25-30 petals), heavy fragrance	Dark; profuse blooms	55, 58, 61, 80, 89, 92
Saratoga (1963) †	White	4″ Double (30-35 petals), heavy fragrance, irregular clusters	Glossy, leathery; vigorous, upright, bushy	77, 80, 92
Spartan (1955)	Orange-red	3-3½″ Double (30 petals), heavy fragrance	Dark, glossy, leathery; disease-resistant	63, 65, 69, 77, 80, 87, 89, 92
The Fairy (1941)*	Pink	1-1½″ Double, no fragrance	Glossy; compact, hardy, spreading	9, 61, 63, 65, 69, 80, 89, 90, 92

*Polyantha   †All-America Rose Selection

Cherry-Vanilla

Prominent

Sunsong

Olé

Aquarius

Introduced in 1950,
Fashion is a floribunda
with the distinction of being
an All-America Rose Selection (right).

Grandifloras

Rose and year of introduction	Color	Flower description	Foliage and growth habits	Catalog sources
Aquarius (1971)†	Pink	4″ Double (30-35 petals), moderately fragrant, long-lasting	Leathery, large; disease-resistant; upright, bushy	55, 61, 77, 86, 92
Arizona (1975)†	Golden copper	4½″ Double, moderately fragrant	Dark, semiglossy; tall plant	10, 22, 55, 58, 61, 62, 65, 69, 79, 80, 86, 87, 89
Buccaneer	Yellow	4″ Double (30 petals), urn-shaped flowers	Glossy foliage; tall-growing	55, 62, 69, 80
Camelot (1964)†	Salmon	3½-4″ Double (40-55 petals), spicy fragrance	Glossy, leathery; moderate blooming	61, 77, 86, 87, 92
Carrousel (1950)	Dark red	3-4″ Semidouble (20 petals), moderately fragrant	Dark, leathery; among the tallest of roses	55, 66, 69, 77, 80, 92
Cherry-Vanilla (1973)	Soft yellow to deep pink	Medium double, moderate tea fragrance	Dark, leathery, semiglossy; very vigorous, upright	10, 55
Comanche (1968)†	Red-orange	3½-4½″ Double, slight fragrance	Leathery; very vigorous, bushy; quick repeat bloomer	22, 65, 77, 87
Montezuma	Terra cotta	4″ Double (30-40 petals)	Leathery, medium-green foliage, tall bushy plant	8, 9, 55, 58, 65, 69 80, 87
Olé (1964)	Orange-red	Medium double (45-55 petals), moderate fragrance	Glossy; vigorous and prolific	55, 61, 77, 80, 86, 89
Prominent (1977)†	Hot orange shaded yellow	3″ Double, slight fragrance, nonfading	Dark; disease-resistant	8, 55, 58, 61, 62, 80, 81, 86, 87, 92
Queen Elizabeth (1954)†	Carmine-rose to dawn-pink	3½-4″ Double (37-40 petals), moderate fragrance	Dark, glossy, leathery; the top-rated grandiflora	9, 10, 18, 22, 55, 58, 61, 62, 65, 69, 77, 80, 82, 86, 87, 89, 92
Scarlet Knight (1966)†	Crimson-scarlet	4-5″ Double, slight fragrance	Leathery; disease-resistant	10, 58, 77, 86, 87, 92
Sonia (1975)	Coral-pink	4″ Double, spicy fragrance	Light green; profuse bloom	58, 65, 69, 79, 86, 89, 92
Sundowner (1978)†	Orange to salmon	4-5″ Double (40 petals), sometimes borne in clusters; spicy fragrance	Moss-green foliage; tall-growing	5, 8, 10, 18, 55, 58, 62, 65, 69, 80, 86, 87, 89, 92

†All-America Rose Selection

Don Juan

America

Tropicana, climbing

Climbers

Rose and year of introduction	Color	Flower description	Foliage and growth habits	Catalog sources
America (1976) †	Coral-pink	4-5" Double, spicy fragrance	Dark, leathery; large-flowered climber; profuse bloom	4, 5, 8, 10, 18, 22, 55, 58, 61, 62, 65, 69, 80, 86, 87, 89, 92
Blaze (1932)	Scarlet	2-3" Semidouble (20 petals), slight fragrance	Dark, leathery; large-flowered climber; easy to grow, thrives everywhere	4, 5, 8, 9, 10, 18, 22, 26, 55, 58, 62, 63, 65, 66, 69, 80, 86, 87, 89, 92
Blossomtime (1951)	Pink	4" Double (35-40 petals), heavy fragrance	Dark; large-flowered climber; low-growing (6 to 7')	66, 92
Crimson Glory, climbing (1946)	Deep crimson to purple	3-4½" Double (30 petals), heavy, spicy fragrance	Leathery; climbing hybrid tea; fast-growing	5, 22, 55, 58, 62, 65, 66, 80, 89, 90
Don Juan (1958)	Dark red	5" Double (35 petals), heavy fragrance, fade-resistant, good cutting	Dark, glossy, leathery; large-flowered climber	5, 10, 22, 55, 58, 61, 63, 65, 69, 77, 80, 87, 89, 92
Dortmund (1955)	Straw-berry-red	2½-3½" Single (5-7 petals), moderate fragrance	Glossy, light green; Kordesii shrub; very vigorous, profuse bloom	61, 62, 90
Doctor J. H. Nicolas (1940)	Rose-pink	5" Double (50 petals), moderate fragrance	Dark, leathery; large-flowered climber; recurrent bloom	9, 63, 65, 80, 92
Golden Showers (1956) †	Daffodil-yellow	4" Double (20-35 petals), moderate fragrance	Dark, glossy; large-flowered climber; long, almost thornless stems	5, 9, 22, 26, 55, 58, 61, 62, 65, 69, 77, 80, 87, 89, 92
Gold Rush (1941)	Gold	Large double (24 petals), moderate fragrance	Glossy; large-flowered climber, not dependably recurrent	9, 65, 80, 90
Handel (1965)	Rose-pink edged cream	3½" Double (22 petals), no fragrance	Glossy, olive-green; large-flowered climber; free-growing, recurrent	61, 77, 92
Heidelberg (1959)	Bright to light crimson	4" Double (52 petals), no fragrance	Glossy, leathery; Kordesii shrub; very vigorous, profuse bloom	77, 90
High Noon, climbing (1946) †	Yellow tinted red	3-4" Double (25-30 petals), spicy fragrance	Glossy, leathery; climbing hybrid tea; vigorous, to 8,' recurrent	55, 80, 85, 86

†All-America Rose Selection

Joseph's Coat

Handel

Rose and year of introduction	Color	Flower description	Foliage and growth habits	Catalog sources
Joseph's Coat (1964)	Yellow and red	3" Double, slight fragrance	Dark, glossy; large-flowered climber; very free-blooming	10, 18, 55, 61, 65, 80, 86, 89
New Dawn (1930)	Pink	2-3" Double, slight fragrance	Dark, glossy; large-flowered climber; continuous blooming, to 20'	26, 55, 69, 89, 92
Paul's Scarlet Climber (1916)	Scarlet	2-3" Semidouble (20 petals), slight fragrance	Dark; large-flowered climber; very hardy and profuse	10, 12, 18, 58, 63, 69, 80
Peace, climbing (1950)	Yellow edged pink	4-5½" Double (40-45 petals), slight fragrance	Dark, glossy, leathery; climbing hybrid tea; shy bloom until established, 15-20'	5, 10, 18, 22, 55, 57, 58, 79, 84, 86, 87, 89, 92
Red Fountain (1975)	Dark red	3" Double, heavy, old-fashioned fragrance	Dark, leathery; large-flowered climber; disease-resistant, 10-12'	9, 58, 69, 80, 92
Rhonda (1968)	Carmine-rose	3-4" Double (40 petals), slight fragrance	Dark, glossy; large-flowered climber; defies bad weather and pests	5, 61, 77, 80, 86, 92
Royal Gold (1957)	Golden yellow	4" Double (30-40 petals), fruity fragrance	Glossy; large-flowered climber; vigorous pillar	8, 58, 77, 80, 86, 89, 92
Show Garden, climbing (1954)	Crimson to rose and magenta	4-5" Double (40-45 petals), no fragrance	Large-flowered climber; free-blooming	9, 10, 12, 18, 63, 65
Talisman, climbing (1930)	Yellow and copper	Medium double (25 petals), moderate fragrance	Glossy, light green; climbing hybrid tea, vigorous plant	5, 8, 80, 86, 89
Tropicana, climbing (1971)	Coral-orange	5" Double (30-35 petals), heavy, fruity fragrance	Dark, glossy; climbing hybrid tea; strong stems produce many blooms	80, 92
Viking Queen (1963)	Medium to deep pink	3-4" Double (60 petals), heavy fragrance	Dark, glossy, leathery; large-flowered climber; profuse, recurrent bloom	9, 12, 92
White Dawn (1949)	White	2-3" Double (35 petals), moderate fragrance, gardenialike blooms	Glossy; large-flowered climber	9, 12, 18, 55, 63, 65, 69, 77, 92

Green Ice

Gold Coin

Beauty Secret

My Valentine

Judy Fischer

Baby Darling

Miniatures

Rose and year of introduction	Color	Flower description	Foliage and growth habits	Catalog sources
Baby Darling (1964)	Orange to orange-pink	1-1½" Double (20 petals), no fragrance	Medium green; bushy growth	72, 73, 74, 75, 76, 78, 84, 86, 92
Baby Gold Star (1940)	Golden yellow	1½-2" Semidouble (12-15 petals), slight fragrance	Medium green; rather large plant	4, 5, 69, 73
Beauty Secret (1965)	Cardinal-red	1-1½" Double, heavy fragrance	Glossy, leathery; abundant bloom	5, 55, 72, 73, 74, 78, 86, 92
Chipper (1966)	Salmon-pink	½-1" Double, slight fragrance	Glossy, leathery; vigorous growth	69, 72, 73, 74, 75, 92
Cricri (1958)	Salmon shaded coral	2" Double (100 petals), no fragrance	Leathery; very bushy, profuse bloom	5, 72, 73, 84, 92
Debbie (1966)	Yellow edged pink	1½" Double, moderate fragrance	Leathery; sometimes semiclimbing	73, 74, 92
Fire Princess (1969)	Orange-red	1¾" Double, no fragrance	Glossy, leathery; vigorous, bushy	72, 73, 74, 75, 79, 84
Gold Coin (1967)	Buttercup-yellow	Small double, moderate fragrance	Dark, leathery; very free bloom	5, 72, 73, 74, 75, 76, 79, 92
Golden Angel (1975)	Deep yellow	Medium double (60-70 petals), sweet fragrance, extra long-lasting cut	Dull green; rounded to spreading	55, 72, 73, 74, 75, 79, 86, 92
Green Ice (1971)	White to green	1½" Double, no fragrance, pink buds	Glossy, leathery, medium green; disease-resistant	72, 73, 74, 75, 76, 78
Hi Ho (1964) †	Light red	Small double, no fragrance	Glossy; vigorous, climbing habit	73, 76, 78, 92
Janna (1970)	Pink, white	1½" Double, no fragrance, long-lasting	Leathery, medium green	72, 73, 74, 75, 76, 78, 92
Jet Trail (1964)	White	Small double (35-45 petals), no fragrance	Medium green; bushy	72, 73, 74, 75, 76
Judy Fischer (1968)	Rose-pink	1½" Double, no fragrance	Bronzy, dark, leathery; low-growing, bushy	72, 73, 74, 75, 76, 78, 92
June Time (1963)	Light pink to dark pink	Small double (75 petals), no fragrance	Glossy; bushy and compact, abundant blooming	12, 72, 73, 74, 75, 78, 84
Kara (1972)	Pink	¾" Single, no fragrance, long-lasting	Medium green; disease-resistant	55, 72, 73, 74, 78
Lavender Lace (1968)	Lavender	1½" Double, moderate fragrance	Glossy; vigorous and bushy	12, 72, 73, 74, 75. 76, 78, 92

†All-America Rose Selection

Lavender Lace

Stacey Sue

Over the Rainbow

Small World

Rose and year of introduction	Color	Flower description	Foliage and growth habits	Catalog sources
Little Curt (1971)	Deep red	1¾" Semidouble to double, no fragrance	Dark, leathery; continuous bloom, disease-resistant	12, 72, 73
Mary Adair (1966)	Apricot	1¾" Double, moderate fragrance	Light green; compact	72, 73, 74, 75, 76
Mary Marshall (1970)	Orange-red, yellow base	1¾" Double, moderate fragrance	Leathery, medium green; disease-resistant, continuous bloom	12, 58, 72, 73, 75, 76, 78, 86, 92
Max Colwell (1975)	Red	1½" Double (20-30 petals), slight fragrance	Leathery, medium green; spreading	55, 72, 73, 75, 92
My Valentine (1975)	Red	1¼" Double, no fragrance	Bronzy, glossy; rounded habit, good for pots	55, 72, 73, 74, 75, 76, 78, 86, 92
Over the Rainbow (1974)	Red and yellow	1¾" Double, slight fragrance	Leathery, medium green; abundant, continuous bloom	72, 73, 74, 75, 76, 78, 92
Persian Princess (1970)	Coral-red	2" Double, moderate fragrance, long-lasting	Leathery, medium green	72, 73, 74
Pink Mandy (1974)	Pink	1" Double (40 petals), no fragrance	Glossy, leathery; low-growing, disease-resistant	72, 73, 74
Shooting Star (1972)	Yellow tipped red	1" Semidouble, slight fragrance	Light green; disease-resistant	73, 74, 84, 92
Small World (1975)	Orange-red	¾" Semidouble (20-22 petals), no fragrance	Glossy, medium green; very compact and rounded	73, 74
Stacey Sue (1976)	Pink	1" Double, no fragrance	Glossy; very bushy	73, 74, 75, 76, 78
Starina (1965)	Orange-scarlet	1½-2" Double, no fragrance, top-rated U.S. rose	Glossy; vigorous, abundant blooming	72, 73, 74, 75, 76, 78, 86, 92
Sweet Fairy (1946)	Apple-blossom pink	¾-1" Double (50-65 petals), moderate fragrance	Dark; moderately compact	5, 73, 76, 77, 78
Toy Clown (1966)	White edged red	1½" Semidouble (20 petals), no fragrance	Leathery; bushy	5, 72, 73, 74, 75, 78, 86, 92
White Angel (1971)	White	1¼" Double, slight fragrance, good exhibition rose	Light green; bushy, profuse blooms	72, 73, 74, 75, 76, 78, 86, 92
Windy City (1974)	Pink	1½" Double, slight fragrance, long-lasting	Bronzy; disease-resistant	72, 73, 74, 92
Yellow Doll (1962)	Yellow to cream	1½" Double (50-60 petals), moderate fragrance, good show rose	Glossy, leathery; vigorous, bushy	12, 55, 72, 73, 75, 76, 78, 84, 92
Yellow Jewel (1973)	Yellow	1½" Semidouble (10 petals), moderate fragrance	Glossy, leathery; bushy, continuous bloom	72, 73, 74, 75, 78

Select Tree Roses Or Elegant Standards

These stately plants are not a class of roses at all, but a distinct garden form. Almost any of the hybrid teas, floribundas, grandifloras, or miniatures listed in these pages can be grown as tree roses (also called standards). Nursery-people simply graft the selected cultivar onto a tall trunk of established root-stock to create this elegant form. The flower and foliage characteristics remain the same as those of the grafted cultivars described in these charts.

Since a chart listing the tree roses available at the time of publication would soon be outdated, we offer you a list of growers who will ship trees. Availability varies from year to year. Check current catalogs for current offerings. In some cases, nurseries will even graft a tree rose especially for you—but you'll have to wait a year or two for the order to be filled.

Standards lend themselves to a variety of landscape uses and are a must for traditional or formal garden design. The older these roses become the more impressive their effect is. They usually need special winter protection (see page 51) and careful pruning (see page 49).

Fragrant Cloud, hybrid tea

Blaze, climbing

Redgold, floribunda

Fire Chief, miniature

Mrs. Sam McGredy, an orange blend hybrid tea, shown here as a tree rose.

Gardeners who overlook roses as a
landscape shrub are missing out on the
possibility for a dramatic display, as
witnessed in this photograph.

ROSES IN YOUR LANDSCAPE

You'll be rewarded with long seasons of blooms for years to come if you incorporate varied forms of roses into your landscape design.

Nature's landscape design has always included roses. According to fossil evidence, they have been around for at least 30 million years. One type of rose or another has grown wild in almost every habitable place in the Northern Hemisphere.

Cultivated roses have an ancient heritage, as well. They were used in the design of Babylon's hanging gardens; they came from Persia to western civilization; the Greeks cultivated rose gardens; and the Romans spread plantings throughout the reaches of their empire.

When the Dark Ages came, the church frowned upon roses, designating "the queen of flowers" as a pagan emblem; but the flowers were kept alive anyway—ironically, in monastery gardens. During the Crusades, more roses were brought back to Europe. And during the Renaissance, the rose, like other things of beauty, was looked upon with favor once again.

But not until the early 19th century, at the time of the Empress Josephine (wife of Napoleon), was the rose restored to its rightful place of honor among flowers. Empress Josephine established extensive gardens at her chateau Malmaison, with plantings of over 250 varieties that included most of the known roses of her day. The fame of these beautiful formal landscapes spread throughout Europe, and soon everyone wanted roses for their own gardens.

Today, the rose is certainly our most popular flower. Over 50 million American families have at least one rose bush under cultivation. The rose is not a part of the total landscape design in most gardens, but is grown primarily for its flowers.

It's unfortunate that roses aren't used more predominantly in landscapes; no other plant produces so many flowers over as long a period of time or has such an astounding variety of plant-growth habits and flower forms.

Roses range from tiny miniatures to towering climbers, and come in all sizes and shapes in between. They can be formed into trees, trained into pillars, grown into huge shrubs, massed together as ground covers, or planted alone as colorful accents. The flowers offer a rainbow of color and an endless variety of sizes and fragrances.

You don't have to wait years for results to show, because most roses bloom the first year they're planted. Few other plants grow under so many different climatic and soil conditions. Best of all, roses are easy to grow; their care hardly requires any time, in comparison to the many rewards they offer.

Designing With Roses

Whether you act as your own landscape architect or use the services of a professional, consider some of the ways roses can fit into your landscape.

☐ Foundation plantings in various heights around the house make the structure look as if it belongs there.

☐ Massed floribundas and miniatures in beds create a lush spot of color against a green lawn. (The plants will be easier to care for if you raise the beds.)

☐ Borders of low-growing roses around flower beds, vegetable gardens, or in front of shrub groupings give long seasons of bloom and make much replanting of bulbs or annuals unnecessary.

☐ Small rose bushes make good accents in rock gardens.

☐ Mobile containers of roses are ideal for patios and terrace gardens, or even for bringing indoors when they're in bloom.

☐ The placement of roses can create optical illusions, leading the eye to another focus, adding extra height, or changing the depth of the lawn.

☐ Formal or casual moods can be created through plant selection and a planting plan.

☐ A grouping of roses or just one large specimen can mark an entryway.

☐ Rose-covered screens give both privacy and beauty.

☐ Roses can form a living fence, hedge, or barrier to block a view, give privacy, or redirect traffic.

☐ Foreground or background plantings of roses emphasize other shrubs and flower companions.

☐ A walkway or path lined with roses invites exploration.

☐ Roses can camouflage fences, unattractive structures, refuse areas, sharp angles, or poorly designed architectural features; and unlike ivy, they won't inflict structural damage.

☐ Well-designed lawns become more interesting when edged with roses.

☐ Colorful blooms can fill in a corner, giving the lawn a completed look.

☐ Proper placement of roses can define and draw attention to a specific area of the landscape.

☐ Plantings that frame a large window at the bottom and sides can bring the rose garden indoors, visually.

☐ Raised or recessed beds built into the patio or terrace bring the roses right into the entertainment area.

☐ Specimen plants of any form of rose, if placed thoughtfully, will accent any spot in the garden.

A circular bed of roses provides a splash of color in the middle of the paved parking area.

☐ Terraced plantings on a steep slope create a wall or bank of flowers.

If you choose to group roses in a "rose garden," you can use a formal or a casual style, either of which can be done on a large or a small scale. It's the design and selection of plants that determines the success of your rose garden.

Formal gardens generally are symmetrical; indeed, the planting patterns often are geometrical. The plants usually follow straight lines, the colors are blended carefully, and often there's some tall feature in the center of the planting—a statue, a pergola, a fountain, or a tree rose—surrounded by roses in descending heights.

Informal gardens, on the other hand, have irregularly spaced plants and flowing lines, resulting in a natural look. More colors and varieties may be combined than in a formal garden, and many other flowers often are planted along with the roses. And why not? Roses blend beautifully with just about any other flower you could name.

Whichever style of rose garden you choose, if you also plant a separate cutting garden, you'll receive two benefits: you'll find it easier to provide the extra care necessary to grow specimen blooms; and you'll be able to leave flowers on the landscape bushes until they fade. Cutting gardens usually are placed out of sight of the public view.

No matter which plant material you use, good designing always requires an understanding of that particular plant's needs and potentials. To determine where to place a given rose bush in your landscape design, study its characteristics and how it is likely to perform. Consider its height, growth habits (bushy, spreading, upright), and foliage type and color. Prune to fit the plant into the design. And remember to choose varieties with long-lasting flowers.

If you want to do your own landscaping, make your plans on paper first. This preliminary step will help you anticipate and avoid many problems that otherwise might require more money, time, and hard work than necessary.

You can learn about landscaping by reading some of the many good books devoted to that art; or you can write your State Cooperative Extension

A mass of low-growing floribundas adds a band of color to divide the green lawn from the cement parking area.

Service (see page 139) for their material on home landscaping. This literature may not discuss roses in particular, but the principles of good rose design are the same as for any other flowering shrub.

Consider Color

Most people feel that all roses blend together in color, but some prefer a more carefully worked-out plan to eliminate color clashes and create harmony. Roses will give you a long, seasonal parade of color, so plan a look you can live with. There's no one way to do it—it's a matter of personal preference and taste. Let your imagination decide what colors will fill your garden.

You may prefer a monochromatic scheme of roses of a single color or several shades of one color. If so, choose a hue that blends well with the materials or color of the house, such as all shades of pink with a pink-toned brick house, or an all-red rose garden to contrast with a white frame house.

You may prefer carefully worked-out blends of two or three colors, using such shades as yellows and oranges planted together, or pinks and reds. Or perhaps you would rather grow two contrasting colors, such as lavender and orange or yellow and red.

If you have enough space, use bold splashes of color in every hue. The resulting riot of color may be more than you want, however, so temper it with a white rose for a quiet accent.

In small areas, mixed colors lose their effectiveness. It's usually best to plant three bushes of the same variety.

Bright, warm colors planted at the rear of the garden make the space appear smaller; cool colors make the garden seem longer or deeper.

Most blooms show best against a background of dark greenery or a dark-painted fence or wall. Some deep rose tones, however, need a light-colored backdrop in order for you to enjoy their rich colors.

Whatever color scheme you work out, plant roses of varying heights to have color at different levels. Use tall-growing grandifloras or climbers for height;

use lower-growing floribundas and miniatures to achieve blooms closer to the ground. Plant height varies within each group of roses; there are short, medium, and tall varieties of hybrid teas, for example.

A Few Words Of Caution

Choose your planting sites carefully. Consider such critical factors as sunshine and good drainage. Give the bushes and roots plenty of room to develop (see pages 18-20).

Buy quality plants. Keep the quantity down to a number you can cope with realistically, depending on how much time and energy you can give. Roses require care all year long in order to produce a season of blooms; so before you begin, be sure you are willing to provide that care. Roses are easy to grow, but they will require at least an hour or so of your time each week.

Remember that roses are deciduous and, for the winter months, will be only naked silhouettes in most landscapes—or, in cold areas, mounds of winter coverings.

Don't overplant. The purpose of good landscaping is to enhance the view, not overwhelm it. And don't forget the view from inside the house looking out.

Above: This house is almost covered with climbing roses and surrounded with an informal rose garden. Top left: Seaside cottages completely entwined with climbing roses have become a tradition on Nantucket Island, Massachusetts. Bottom left: Climbing polyantha, Mme. Cécile Brunner, frames this old-fashioned picture-postcard entrance gate.

Consider Planting Tradition

Using roses "traditionally" in the landscape may mean something different to each of you. Perhaps your first image is of the formal garden style, typical of European estates since the days of Empress Josephine.

Or maybe you hold a romantic vision of the proverbial rose-covered cottage, a favorite red climber spreading over a whitewashed picket fence, or even trim rows of rose bushes standing at attention in an isolated rose bed.

When you plan your landscape design, think about including some of the best elements from our rose-garden heritage that fit into your own surroundings and life style.

Try Something Different

Don't restrict your roses to the rose garden. Give these handsome, hardy plants a chance to perform varied landscape duties. They are far more versatile than they're often given credit for. Place them in the foreground or background to perform as a colorful star or to blend subtly alongside annuals, bulbs, other shrubs, or even vegetables.

The true rosarian is not afraid to experiment—whether it's with new varieties, new methods of culture, or new landscape possibilities. There are quite a few good ideas and successful garden designs presented in the following pages and throughout this book.

Small Landscape Gem

Don and Mary Marshall are both Consulting Rosarians for the American Rose Society and are active rose show judges. When you approach their home, you can tell that the owners love roses. Their garden is an excellent example of good landscaping with roses, as the illustrations at left show.

The Marshalls have been growing prize-winning roses at their San Mateo, California home for about 30 years. Their relatively small yard contains over 350 rose plants, but an organized sense of design creates a harmonious rather than chaotic effect. Since both Marshalls work daily, they can do their garden chores only in the early morning and on weekends.

In 1970, rose breeder Ralph Moore named one of his best miniature varieties for Mary Marshall.

Top: The lawn becomes a bouquet of blooms on all levels. Above: Climbing Shot Silk covers an extension to the rear of the house. Right: This weeping Margo Koster tree rose is formed with the aid of a wire frame.

Above: A formal pergola is adorned with the "thousand beauties rose," Tausendschön, 1906.

All photos on this page show the Huntington Botanical rose gardens' beautiful landscape design that blends formal tradition with informal English country gardens, using both old roses and new.

Top: Miniature rose Sunny Day grows successfully as a hanging basket plant. Bottom: Container-grown roses can be grouped together to provide colorful gardens wherever they are desired.

The Mobile Rose Garden

When you grow roses in containers, you are totally free to change the design of your landscape—for special occasions, according to changes in the weather, or just on a whim.

Miniatures are obvious container-garden candidates—but full-sized roses, even climbers and trees, also can be grown and moved in large pots or tubs successfully (see pages 23, 26-27).

For people who have only limited space, balconies, decks, or terraces, yet who still want to grow roses, container gardening is the answer.

An Urban Highrise Garden

A rose garden in the sky is not some romantic daydream but a fact of life for gardening writer Linda Yang. Her very real garden is nestled on two terraces of a modern highrise apartment building.

Ms. Yang had long admired roses but assumed that they could be grown only in country gardens. She decided to give terrace gardening a try, however, and in spite of discouragement from nurserypeople, she has added the queen of flowers to her garden, using trial and error as her teacher.

Her secret is to start with plants that already are growing in cardboard containers. She avoids buying bare-root roses; transplanting causes too much shock for rooftop growing. She makes her selections at local nurseries and waits until midspring to transplant her roses into her large containers.

Left: Climbing Don Juan and floribunda
Gene Boerner team up for a refreshing
contrast to the concrete city below.
Below: A screen provides intimacy as well
as protection from harsh city winds
and noises.

One terrace conveys a feeling of slight formality. A long planter and screen of dark green *treillage* form the background for climbing roses. The screen also provides privacy from adjoining highrises and protection from cold winds, without blocking the great view of the park. Ivy is a natural choice for ground cover in such a setting. Tree roses in boxes near the apartment windows offer an eye-level splash of summer color.

The garden design of the other terrace is quite informal. Climbing roses trained on a wire fence frame the cityscape and soften the harshness of adjacent buildings. Floribundas planted at the bases of the climbers give rose blooms on all levels.

Hybrid teas and more climbers in large tubs are used as accent plants. Apparently, they do not object to sharing these tubs with small but compatible woody shrubs, such as cotoneaster and pyracantha, or with an everchanging display of annuals—alyssum, marigolds, and zinnias.

Ms. Yang's family and friends enjoy her skyline rose garden as a retreat from noisy city streets as well as an outdoor dining area. Outdoor lighting creates a pleasant, dramatic effect at night when the terrace is viewed from inside the apartment—quite an unexpected treat for guests anticipating just another city view.

When The Accent Is On Roses

Sometimes the key word in landscaping is *restraint*. A single strategically placed rosebush can be enough to: act as a bold accent in the garden design; serve as a focal point or dominant element; call attention to a particular area; or add interest to a lawn, flower bed, or grouping of shrubs.

When a rose stands alone, it should be special, a perfect example of its type. Whether it's a large shrub species, a tree or standard, a spectacular climber, or an unusual-colored hybrid tea, its placement should be such that it can be viewed as an individual rosebush or a stand-out among the other plants in its area. Naturally, such a prominent plant must always be healthy and well groomed.

Visit A Public Rose Garden

You can learn a great deal by visiting public rose gardens: you can discover landscape-design ideas, see new introductions and tests, preview future All-America Rose Selections, smell and touch unusual or hard-to-find varieties, and study old-fashioned species. All show off their best qualities in response to the particular climate of the garden.

In the public rose gardens, look for roses you like. Observe their growing habits to see how the plants might fit your own landscape needs. Let specimen blooms guide you in selecting the color, fragrance, and size you want for your own cutting garden. Jot down the names so you can order or find the desired species or variety later on. Seek out the resident horticulturist, who usually is happy to answer any serious questions.

We've included a sampling of some of the 250 North American public rose gardens. A complete list, with addresses, is available from All-America Rose Selections, P.O. Box 218, Shenandoah, Iowa 51610.

In addition, many commercial rose growers have display gardens at their home offices. Check the list on page 140. Call ahead to be sure they have areas open to the public.

Top: A specimen tree rose stands sentinel near an entrance and offers a splash of color to enrich the plain brick wall. Middle: The focal point in the corner of this lawn is a brilliantly hued climber entwined around the gaslight. Bottom: Rose Hills Memorial Park, Whittier, CA. Above: Brooklyn Botanic Garden, Brooklyn, NY.

Public Rose Gardens

United States

California
Arcadia, County Park Rose Garden
Berkeley, Municipal Rose Garden
Fresno, Municipal Rose Garden
La Canada, Descanso Gardens
Los Angeles, Exposition Park Rose Garden
Oakland, Morcum Amphitheater of Roses
Riverside, Fairmont Park Rose Garden
Sacramento, Capitol Park Rose Garden
San Diego, Balboa Park
San Jose, Municipal Rose Garden
San Marino, Huntington Botanical Gardens
Santa Barbara, City Rose Garden and Armory
  Gardens
Visalia, Tulare County Courthouse
Westminister, Civic Center Rose Garden
Whittier, Rose Hills Memorial Park

Colorado
Denver, Denver Botanic Gardens
Longmont, Memorial Rose Garden

Connecticut
Norwich, Memorial Rose Garden
Waterbury, Hamilton Park Rose Garden
West Hartford, Elizabeth Park Rose Garden

Florida
Cypress Gardens, Cypress Gardens

Georgia
Atlanta, Greater Atlanta Rose Garden,
  Piedmont Park

Hawaii
Kula, University of Hawaii, College of Tropical
  Agriculture

Idaho
Boise, Julia Davis Park
Lewiston, Memorial Bridge Rose Garden

Illinois
Chicago, Grant Park Rose Garden and
  Marquette Park Rose Garden
Highland Park, Gardener's Memorial Garden
Libertyville, Cook Memorial Rose Garden
Peoria, Park District Rose Garden, Glen Oak
  Park Conservatory
Wheaton, Robert R. McCormick Memorial
  Gardens

Indiana
Fort Wayne, Lakeside Park Rose Garden
Richmond, E. G. Hill Memorial Rose Garden,
  Glen Miller Park

Iowa
Ames, Iowa State University Rose Garden
Bettendorf, Community Center Rose Garden
Cedar Rapids, Huston Park Rose Garden
Davenport, Van der Veer Park Municipal
  Rose Garden
Muscatine, Weed Park Memorial Rose
  Garden
Shenandoah, Mount Arbor Demonstration
  Garden
Waterloo, Byrnes Park Memorial Rose
  Garden

Kansas
Manhattan, Kansas State University Rose
  Garden
Topeka, E. F. A. Reinisch Rose and Test
  Garden, Gage Park

Kentucky
Louisville, Kentucky Memorial Rose Garden

Louisiana
Baton Rouge, L.S.U. Rose Test Garden
Many, Hodges Gardens
New Orleans, Pauline Worthington Memorial
  Rose Garden, City Park
Shreveport, American Rose Center

Massachusetts
Westfield, The Stanley Park

Michigan
East Lansing, Michigan State University
  Horticulture Gardens
Lansing, Francis Park Memorial Rose Garden

Minnesota
Duluth, Duluth Rose Garden
Minneapolis, Municipal Rose Garden

Missouri
Cape Girardeau, Rose Display Garden,
  Capaha Park
Kansas City, Blue Ridge Mall Rose Garden
  and Laura Conyers Smith Memorial Rose
  Garden
St. Louis, Missouri Botanical Rose Garden

Montana
Missoula, Memorial Rose Garden, Sunset
  Park

Nebraska
Lincoln, Municipal Rose Garden
Omaha, Memorial Park Rose Garden

Nevada
Reno, Municipal Rose Garden, Idlewild Park

New Jersey
Bloomfield, Brookdale Park Rose Garden
East Millstone, Colonial Park Rose Garden

New Mexico
Albuquerque, Prospect Park Rose Garden
Hobbs, Community Rose Garden, Lea
  General Hospital

New York
Brooklyn, Cranford Memorial Rose Garden,
  Brooklyn Botanic Garden
Buffalo, Niagara Frontier Trial Rose Garden,
  Humboldt Park
Flushing, Queens Botanical Garden
Ithaca, Cornell University Rose Garden
Newark, The National Rose Garden
New York, United Nations Rose Garden
Rochester, Maplewood Rose Garden
Schenectady, Central Park Rose Garden

North Carolina
Raleigh, Municipal Rose Garden

Ohio
Columbus, Park of Roses and Ohio State
  University Rose Garden
Mansfield, Kingwood Center
Wooster, Ohio Agricultural Research Center

Oklahoma
Muskogee, J. E. Conard Municipal Rose
  Garden, Honor Heights Park
Oklahoma City, Municipal Rose Garden,
  Will Rogers Park
Tulsa, Municipal Rose Garden, Woodard Park

Oregon
Corvallis, Municipal Rose Garden, Avery Park
Eugene, George E. Owen Municipal Rose
  Garden
Portland, International Rose Test Garden

Pennsylvania
Allentown, Malcolm W. Gross Memorial
  Rose Garden
Hershey, Rose Gardens and Arboretum
Kennett Square, Longwood Gardens
McKeesport, Renziehausen Park Arboretum
Pittsburgh, Mellon Park Rose Gardens
Reading, Municipal Rose Garden
University Park, Penn State University
  Rose Garden

South Carolina
Orangeburg, Edisto Rose Garden

Tennessee
Chattanooga, Municipal Rose Garden, Warner
  Park
Memphis, Municipal Rose Garden, Audubon
  Park

Texas
Corpus Christi, Rose Society Display Garden
Dallas, Samuell-Grand Municipal Rose
  Garden
El Paso, Municipal Rose Garden
Fort Worth, Botanic Garden
Houston, Municipal Rose Garden
San Angelo, Municipal Rose Garden, Civic
  League Park
Tyler, Rose Garden Park

Utah
Fillmore, Territorial Statehouse Rose Garden,
  Old Capitol State Park
Nephi, Municipal Memorial Rose Garden
Salt Lake City, Municipal Rose Garden

Virginia
Arlington, Memorial Rose Garden
Roanoke, Mountain View Garden

Washington
Bellingham, Fairhaven Park Rose Garden
Chehalis, Municipal Rose Garden
Seattle, Woodland Park Rose Garden
Spokane, Rose Hill, Manito Park
Tacoma, Point Defiance Park Rose Garden

West Virginia
Huntington, Ritter Park Rose Garden

Wisconsin
Hales Corners, Boerner Botanical Garden,
  Whitnall Park
Madison, Olbrich Park

Public Rose Gardens

Canada

British Columbia
Victoria, The Butchart Gardens

Ontario
Niagara Falls, Royal Horticultural Gardens
Windsor, Jackson Park Rose Garden

Quebec
Montreal, Connaught Park Rose Garden and
  Memorial Park Rose Garden

CREATING NEW ROSES

Try your hand at hybridizing— create a new rose. All you need are a few blooms, a bit of luck, and a lot of patience.

The rating of 10.0 is the highest any rose can achieve—it signifies a *Perfect* rose. But if you check the results of the American Rose Society's annual survey to establish ratings for all roses currently available in the United States, you'll notice that not one single rose is perfect by these standards.

In fact, out of almost 1,300 roses listed, only two hybrid teas, one grandiflora, two miniatures, two shrubs, and seven old garden roses rate 9.0 or above —the *Outstanding* class. (See rating scale and list of top roses on pages 92-93.)

Today's roses are the result of centuries of genetic reshuffling—the combined work of both nature and man. Hybridizers have combined and recombined genes for constant improvement. This attempt to reach perfection has brought forth new colors, forms, textures, habits, and fragrances, as well as more vigor and disease resistance.

Nevertheless, a large degree of luck is involved. Nature remains boss; and occasionally she reminds us of that fact by producing something totally new or unexpected.

Most of the roses currently on the world market have been produced by the work of about 50 professional hybridizers. Each one cross-pollinates thousands of roses per year in the hope of finding that "perfect" one. The number of possible genetic combinations for new roses is stupefying, but the odds are about 10,000 to 1 against any specific cross-fertilization producing an outstanding new rose.

These 50 or so professional rosarians have no corner on rose development, however; numerous amateurs try their hand, too, and some of them are able to come up with a good rose—one that becomes a commercial success, even an award winner.

Carl Meyer, a pipe fitter, experimented for 7 years before coming up with what he considered a worthy seedling. Then, after 4 more years of testing, Star Roses released Meyer's creation as 'Portrait'. The rose underwent still another 2 years of tests before it was named the All-America Rose Selection in 1972.

Perhaps the "perfect" rose will never be recognized. Perfection, after all, is an elusive quality. What one person may consider most desirable in a rose, another may not appreciate. Elusive or not, however, the search for the perfect rose goes on.

How do you measure perfection? You must be able to recognize something worth developing when it comes up. Does it have something unique to offer? Are there qualities in color, form, or fragrance that make your rose superior to others? It's possible that many "perfect" roses have been discarded by other breeders who could not see the attributes when they were there.

Your chance to join in the search for the perfect rose is as close as your rose garden, and to begin is as simple as the steps outlined on the next two pages. Be careful though—you may find yourself on the path to an all-consuming hobby.

1. Remove the outer petals of selected parents to expose the flower's reproductive organs.

2. In the center are pistils, surrounded by stamens that are tipped with pollen-bearing anthers.

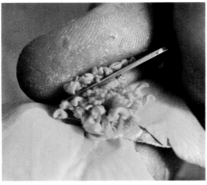

3. Remove the anthers from both parents before they ripen, open, and self-pollinate the rose.

4. Store anthers from the chosen male inside a labeled container and allow to dry.

How To Create A New Rose

All roses are bisexual. Nature has provided each rose with both stamens (male organs) and pistils (female organs) for self-pollination. You hybridize roses by taking the pollen from the stamens on the flower of one plant and applying it to the pistils on the flower of another. The process begins early in the rose season to allow plenty of time for the fruit to mature before dormancy sets in again.

The parental role depends on whether a rose is chosen to *provide* the pollen or *receive* it. Since it seems to be a tossup as to which parent has the greater influence in transmitting its characteristics, expert hybridizers make reciprocal crossings, using the same variety for both the male and the female.

You can see both sets of reproductive organs if you remove the flower petals from a rose carefully. The very center contains the pistils—delicate stalks connected to an ovary at the bottom end and to a pollen-receiving stigma at the tip.

Surrounding the pistils are the stamens. These are slender stalks tipped by the anthers—kernel-like sacs that hold the pollen. The first phase of hybridization is to emasculate both parents. Even if you are using a particular rose as a female, you must remove its anthers before they have a chance to open and self-pollinate the rose. Remove the petals from partially opened buds, and pluck the anthers off with tweezers or cut them with a sharp knife. Be careful not to damage the pistils.

Place the anthers gathered from the male-designated rose in a closed jar, where they can dry. Date and identify according to variety. You can discard the flower that furnished the pollen, or you can use it as a female in a simultaneous experiment.

In a day or so, the anthers inside the jar will ripen and open (dehisce), releasing their dustlike pollen grains. These grains actually are minute capsules that contain the sperm.

During this time, the female parent prepares to receive the pollen. When the female's stigmas are tipped with a sticky secretion, you know it is time for the pollination.

Brush all the dry pollen onto the receptive stigmas with an artist's camelhair brush. The secretion of the stigma not only makes the pollen adhere but also dissolves the capsule, thus releasing the tiny sperm. The pollen then sends down tiny, hairlike pollen tubes through the stalks to an ovary containing unfertilized eggs. There, a male reproductive cell unites with an egg.

Once the crossing is complete, label the female flower to identify the varieties that served as the parents. Tie a bag (paper, glassine, or plastic) over the flower to protect it from dust or unwanted pollen. At this point, your task is just to wait—it's up to nature now. Have patience, and don't be disappointed if it doesn't work. The percentage of successful fertilizations is low.

If the pollination fails to take, the hip will dry up and fall off the plant. If the pollination does take, the hip will stay green and swell with growth within a few weeks.

It takes about 2½ months for the seed hips to ripen. Then they turn bright orange, yellow, red, or brown, depending upon the variety or species. Gather the hips (along with the label) when they first turn color, before they become overripe. Fresh seeds tend to germinate faster.

Next, slice the hip carefully with a knife, expose the seeds, and remove them. There may be only 1 seed or as many as 50.

Condition (stratify) the seeds by storing them in polyethylene bags of peat moss. Refrigerate at 40°F. for about 6 weeks.

When you remove the seeds from refrigeration, plant them according to the seed propagation procedure outlined on page 35.

The first flowers may appear 7 to 8 weeks after germination. This is the first indication of your results. Now you must decide, according to your personal preference, whether to leave the seedlings to develop for further testing or to discard them.

5. In about a day a sticky secretion appears on the stigma as an indication that it is pollen-receptive.

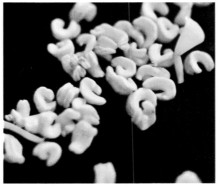

6. At about the same time, the anthers release their dustlike pollen grains containing the sperm.

7. Using a small, soft brush, place the dried pollen onto the female's sticky-coated stigma.

8. Label the pollinated bud and cover it with a glassine bag for protection against dust and unwanted pollen.

9. If pollination is successful, the hip will swell with growth as in the fertile hip on the right.

10. Sometimes seeds are borne on the outside of the hip. Harvest about 2½ months after the crossing.

11. When the hip has matured and turned color, cut it carefully with a small sharp knife.

12. Divide the hip into sections and peel them open to reveal the seeds that have developed.

13. Stratify the seeds by placing them in peat moss and storing at 40° F. for up to six weeks.

14. Plant seeds in a very loose growing medium and wait for germination. This seedling is 1 week old.

15. Evaluate the results of your cross and weed out seedlings that are weak or have poor color.

16. Label the most promising seedlings for continued development and budding at the end of the summer.

At the end of summer, a seedling will be ready to be budded onto rootstock for extensive testing, propagation, and evaluation (see page 36).

If you think you've come up with the perfect rose—or at least a good one—send one of your seedlings to a respected commercial rose grower. Be sure and correspond with the grower before you ship your plant. (See catalog listing, page 140). The grower will evaluate your results and possibly purchase the rights for development and distribution.

You may benefit from membership in the Rose Hybridizers Association. For details, write to Mr. Pete Haring, Fox Hill Lane, Box 35, Stony Brook, NY 11790.

The Testing Period

A rose hybridizer must be patient. It may take 10 years or more between the birth of a new rose and its official public introduction. Once it has been bred successfully, the rose becomes merely a number in a commercial rose grower's test garden, where it will receive rigorous testing.

A typical rose company examines seedlings of as many as 600 different new roses per year. Ninety-five percent of these originate within the company or with professional hybridizers. From these seedlings, about 25 to 30 will be deemed worthy of further observation. Out of these, a dozen or so will be retained for more trials, and may be grown for as long as 5 years. Ultimately, only 4 or 5 of these will have passed all the tests well enough to be introduced to the public.

Protecting Your Investment

Until the Townsend-Purnell Plant Patent Act was passed in 1930, a hybridizer could go through the process of developing a new rose without ever reaping any financial benefits. A plant could be propagated by anyone as soon as it was released.

Today, however, the Plant Patent Act protects the inventor of plants, just as the originator of industrial inventions is protected.

"Whoever invents or discovers and asexually reproduces any distinct and new variety of plant, including cultivated sports, mutants, hybrids, and newly formed seedlings . . . may obtain a patent therefore subject to the conditions and requirements of this title."

The patent owner receives legal protection for 17 years. During that time, the owner receives a royalty for every offspring of his or her plant. This helps

Ralph Moore, owner of Sequoia Nursery of Visalia, California, has been a pioneer in miniature roses and certainly one of America's most prolific rose breeders.

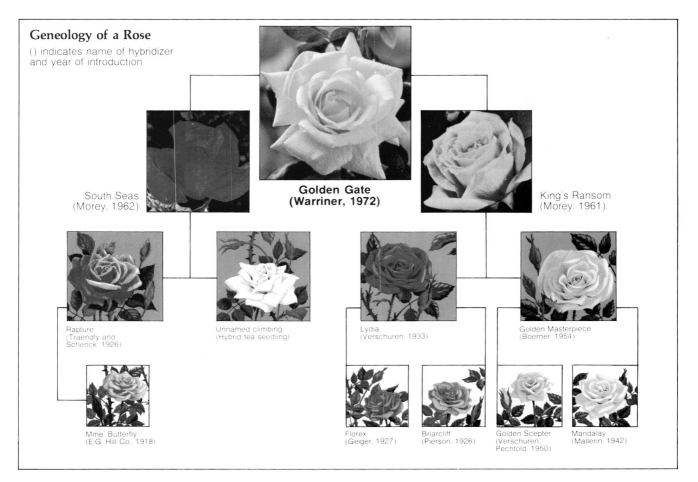

Geneology of a Rose

() indicates name of hybridizer
and year of introduction

**Golden Gate
(Warriner, 1972)**

South Seas
(Morey. 1962)

King's Ransom
(Morey. 1961)

Rapture
(Traendly and
Schenck. 1926)

Unnamed climbing
(Hybrid tea seedling)

Lydia
(Verschuren. 1933)

Golden Masterpiece
(Boerner. 1954)

Mme. Butterfly
(E.G. Hill Co., 1918)

Florex
(Geiger. 1927)

Briarcliff
(Pierson. 1926)

Golden Scepter
(Verschuren.
Pechtold. 1950)

Mandalay
(Mallerin. 1942)

to recoup the investment cost and maybe even show a profit for all the effort. Commercial rose nurseries can purchase the patent rights from the inventor and receive enough return to compensate for the expensive publicity necessary to introduce the new rose.

All patented roses are required to have a metal tag attached. This is your guarantee of the plant variety and quality. Avoid buying roses sold as "patented" unless they wear this identification tag with patent number.

During these years of testing, the roses are judged for petal count, color, fragrance, foliage, disease resistance, and other factors important to the rosarian.

Since roses introduced to the public represent considerable investment in growing space, time, labor, and promotion, the commercial rose nurseries must select those that will do well nationally under various conditions.

In addition to their own test gardens, reliable rose companies rely on test panels or test gardens throughout the country to field test the roses being considered. The following comments on why certain roses were dropped from further testing come from one of these companies:

"C65-8031: Although this rose seemed to have great merit in our test gardens, nationwide tests indicated that its cycle between blooming periods was too long. . . .

"66-11533: Plant made poor comeback after first bloom. . . .

"C66-7591: Awkward habit. . . .

"C64-5182: Proved to be nonvigorous in many regions. The color, although pleasing, faded too quickly in many climates. . . .

"C63-3937: Geographical variance in plant performance and disease resistance. . . .

"58-6103: Unstable color. . . ."

When breeding your own roses, it's a good idea to keep this type of criticism in mind—it can help you pre-qualify a rose before putting it before others.

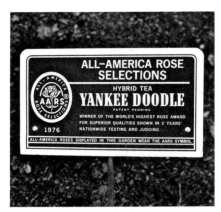

AARS signs are proudly displayed in public rose gardens.

What's In A Name?

Once a rose is ready for its public debut, it will need a name. The hybridizer or distributing nursery registers the name with the American Rose Society, which has been designated as our National Rose Registration Center by the International Registration Authority for Roses.

The registration center reviews the chosen name, which is accompanied by complete descriptions, and rejects names that do not conform to provisions of the International Code. Nonacceptable names include those that are too similar to existing roses. It is possible to reuse a name after 30 years, if proof can be supplied that the original rose is extinct, is not of historical importance, or was not used as a parent of an existing cultivar.

All-America Rose Selections

Unfortunately, the 1930 Plant Patent Act only requires that a plant be different in some respect from existing plants. Therefore, within a short time after this enactment, patents were granted to many roses of inferior quality and performance. The public was paying a higher price for merchandise of questionable quality.

Rose people knew that something had to be done to test the merits of new roses before they were offered to the public, so in 1938 the All-America Rose Selections was born. This nonprofit organization tests new rose originations, gives recognition in the form of an All-America award to the new rose candidates that have proved outstanding in 2-year trials, and acquaints the press and gardening public of the United States and Canada with the award-winning roses.

Over the years, AARS has been effective enough to earn the confidence of the buying public—40 percent of the total sales of roses today are All-America winners. In a recent poll of the American public to pick its favorite rose, all 10 of the finalists were former All-America winners. Incidentally, America's favorite rose was 'First Prize', followed closely by 'Peace'.

There are 26 official AARS Test Gardens scattered in 19 states throughout the nation. Most are located at universities or large public rose gardens. They are maintained rigidly by AARS standards.

Anyone may enter the All-America competition by paying an entry fee and furnishing trial plants for the gardens. The roses are subjected to 2 years of testing by well-trained judges. Only cultivars scoring in first or second place in their classes are even considered by the membership for the coveted awards.

These four famous All-America Selections are still top-rated in national testing by the American Rose Society: First Prize, AARS 1970; Tiffany, AARS 1955, Queen Elizabeth, AARS 1955; Peace, AARS 1946.

Roses that are not winners but receive high scores normally are introduced anyway by the firms submitting them. Those with relatively low scores usually are dropped. This not only greatly reduces the total number of varieties introduced but also ensures that higher-quality new cultivars will be marketed than in the past.

Other Awards For Roses

Although the AARS brings the most prestige and financial return to a new rose, a number of other prestigious awards are given to well-tested roses. These include:

Bagatelle Gold Medal (Paris)
Geneva Gold Medal
Madrid Gold Medal
Portland (Oregon) Gold Medal
Rome Gold Medal

Royal National Rose Society of
  Great Britain Gold Medal
The Hague Gold Medal
  and Golden Rose

The American Rose Society also gives a number of awards, including the National Gold Medal Certificate.

There's even a special award for rose fragrance. The James Alexander Gamble Rose Fragrance Medal is granted by the American Rose Foundation. Currently, only 8 roses have been honored with this award:

'Crimson Glory' (1961)
'Tiffany' (1962)
'Chrysler Imperial' (1965)
'Sutter's Gold' (1966)

'Granada' (1968)
'Fragrant Cloud' (1970)
'Papa Meilland' (1974)
'Sunsprite' (1979)

Winners of ARS National Gold Medal Certificates

'Peace' (1948)
'City of York' (1950)
'Carrousel' (1954)
'Fashion' (1954)
'Frensham' (1955)
'Vogue' (1956)
'Chrysler Imperial' (1956)

'Golden Wings' (1958)
'Queen Elizabeth' (1960)
'Montezuma' (1961)
'Spartan' (1961)
'Tropicana' (1967)
'Toy Clown' (1971)

The Proof Of The Pudding

Probably one of the most meaningful tests of roses is the national survey that the ARS does each year to determine the quality of roses grown by its members in their home gardens. These ratings, called "Proof of the Pudding," are based on the gardening experiences and opinions of many of the members of the American Rose Society who actually have grown the roses in question.

Roses remain on the checklist for 3 years to establish a rating. Comments and opinions are sent to district reporters throughout the country. They compile the results and send their findings to the ARS. The final tabulation is a composite of reports from all parts of the nation.

You can keep abreast of new additions or yearly changes in the ratings by annually ordering a copy of the *Handbook for Selecting Roses* from the American Rose Society, Box 30,000, Shreveport, LA 71130, at a cost of 35¢.

Here is a list of the roses that have been rated at least 8.0. Note the large number of old roses and shrubs that stay right up there with the new cultivars. It's also interesting to see that the highest rated rose is a miniature, 'Starina'.

Roses used in the landscape don't have to be numerous or massive in size to command attention. This single well-groomed species combines colorfully with iris at left. Note the contrast of the giant pink blossoms against the expanse of green lawn.

National Rating Scale:

10.0	Perfect	7.9 - 7.0	Good
9.9 - 9.0	Outstanding	6.9 - 6.0	Fair
8.9 - 8.0	Excellent	5.9 and lower	Of questionable value

Highest-rated Roses

Old garden roses
'Celsiana' (D) 9.3
R. gallica officinalis (G) 9 3
R. Banksiae (Sp) 9.1
R. hugonis (Sp) 9.1
Rosa Mundi (G) 9.1
R. banksiae banksiae (Sp) 9.0
'Rose de Rescht' (D) 9.0
'Mme. Hardy' (D) 8.8
R. chinensis mutabilis (Sp) 8.8
'Tricolore de Flandre' (G) 8.8
'Charles de Millis' (G) 8.7
Common Moss (M) 8.7
Crested Moss (M) 8.7
'Sombreuil' (T) 8.6
'Jacques Cartier' (P) 8.5
'Souvenir de la Malmaison' (B) 8.5
'Celina' (M) 8.4
'Tuscany' (G) 8.4
'William Lobb' (M) 8.4
'General Kleber' (M) 8.3
'Mabel Morrison' (HO) 8.3
'Mme. Ernst Calvat' (B) 8.3
'Oskar Cordel' (HP) 8.3
'Paul's Early Blush' (HP) 8.3
'Rose de Meaux' (C) 8.3
'Serratipetala' (Ch) 8.3
'Mrs. John Laing' (HP) 8.2
'La Reine Victoria' (B) 8.1
'York and Lancaster' (D) 8.1
'Commandant Beaurepaire' (B) 8.0
'Crimson Globe' (M) 8.0
'Leda' (D) 8.0
'Marie Louise' (D) 8.0
R. foetida bicolor (Sp) 8.0
R. moschata (Sp) 8.0
R. nitida (Sp) 8.0
'Salet' (M) 8.0
'Stanwell Perpetual' (HSpn) 8.0
'Tuscany Superb' (G) 8.0
'Waldfee' (HP) 8.0

A—*Alba*
B—*Bourbon*
C—*Centifolia*
Ch—*China*
D—*Damask*
G—*Gallica*
HFt—*Hybrid Foetida*
HP—*Hybrid Perpetual*
HSpn—*Hybrid Spinosissima*
M—*Moss*
N—*Noisette*
P—*Portland*
Sp—*Species*
T—*Tea*

Shrubs
'Cornelia' (HMsk) 9.1
'Dortmund' (K) 9.1
'Frau Dagmar Hastrup' (HRg) 8.9
'Pink Grootendorst' (HRg) 8.9
'Will Scarlet' (HMsk) 8.8
'Nastarana' (HMsk) 8.6
'Applejack' 8.5
'Belinda' (HMsk) 8.5
'Blanc Double de Coubert' (HRg) 8.5
'F. J. Grootendorst' (HRg) 8.5
'Golden Wings' 8.5
'Hansa' (HRg) 8.5
'Ruskin' (HRg) 8.5
'Flamingo' (HRg) 8.3
'Alchymist' 8.2
'Dronroschen' 8.2
'Nevada' (HM) 8.2
R. rugosa 'Alba' 8.2
R. rugosa 'Rubra' 8.2
'Cerise Bouquet' 8.1
'Prairie Star' 8.1
'Canterbury' 8.0
'Carefree Beauty' 8.0
'Summer Wind' 8.0

HMoy—*Hybrid Moyesii*
HMsk—*Hybrid Musk*
Hrg—*Hybrid Rugosa*
K—*Kordesii*

Hybrid teas
'First Prize' 9.1
'Dainty Bess' 8.8
'Double Delight' 8.8
'Tiffany' 8.8
'Garden Party' 8.7
'Granada' 8.7
'Miss All-American Beauty' 8.7
'Mister Lincoln' 8.7
'Century Two' 8.6
'Swarthmore' 8.6
'Lady X' 8.5
'Peace' 8.5
'Royal Highness' 8.5
'Nantucket' 8.4
'Pascali' 8.4
'Tropicana' 8.4
'Chicago Peace' 8.3
'Chrysler Imperial' 8.1
'Electron' 8.1
'Fragrant Cloud' 8.1
'Just Joey' 8.1
'Color Magic' 8.0
'Confidence' 8.0
'Duet' 8.0
'Feuerzauber' 8.0
'Folklore' 8.0
'Lemon Sherbet' 8.0
'Lustige' 8.0
'Maria Stern' 8.0
'Paradise' 8.0
'Precious Platinum' 8.0
'Pristine' 8.0
'Red Jacket' 8.0

Miniatures
'Starina' 9.4
'Beauty Secret' 9.3
'Magic Carrousel' 8.9
'Toy Clown' 8.9
'Judy Fischer' 8.8
'Kathy Robinson' 8.8
'Simplex' 8.8
'Cinderella' 8.7
'Hi Ho' 8.7
'Mary Marshall' 8.7
'Kathy' 8.6
'Starglo' 8.6
'Top Secret' 8.6
'Baby Darling' 8.5
'Holy Toledo' 8.5
'Over the Rainbow' 8.5
'Rise 'n' Shine' 8.5
'Rosmarin' 8.5
'Janna' 8.4
'White Angel' 8.4
'Yellow Doll' 8.4
'Baby Betsy McCall' 8.3
'Jeanie Lajoie' 8.3
'Willie Winkie' 8.3
'Opal Jewel' 8.2
'Sheri Anne' 8.2
'Petite Folie' 8.1
'Popcorn' 8.1
'Robin' 8.1
'Baby Katie' 8.0
'Chattem Centennial' 8.0
'Chipper' 8.0
'Cuddles' 8.0
'Dreamglo' 8.0

'Gloriglo' 8.0
'Heidi' 8.0
'Lavender Jewel' 8.0
'Mary Adair' 8.0
'Orange Honey' 8.0
'Pacesetter' 8.0
'Peaches 'n Cream' 8.0
'Pink Mandy' 8.0
'Pink Petticoat' 8.0
'Puppy Love' 8.0
'Red Flush' 8.0
R. rouletti 8.0
'Rose Hills Red' 8.0
'Snow Magic' 8.0
'Stars 'n' Stripes' 8.0
'Swedish Doll' 8.0

Polyanthas
'The Fairy' 8.6
'China Doll' 8.0

Climbers
'Altissimo' 8.0
'Galway Bay' 8.7
'Cecile Brunner' 8.3
'Don Juan' 8.3
'Royal Flush' 8.3
'America' 8.2
'Royal Sunset' 8.1
'Blossomtime' 8.0
'Dainty Bess' 8.0
'Dublin Bay' 8.0
'Lawrence Johnston' 8.0
'New Dawn' 8.0
'Pinata' 8.0

Floribundas
'Iceberg' 8.9
'Little Darling' 8.9
'Europeana' 8.8
'Sunfire' 8.8
'Gene Boerner' 8.7
'Ivory Fashion' 8.7
'Sea Pearl' 8.7
'Betty Prior' 8.5
'Evening Star' 8.5
'First Edition' 8.4
'Matador' 8.2
'Escapade' 8.1
'Liverpool Echo' 8.1
'Orange Sensation' 8.1
'Anabell' 8.0
'Angel Face' 8.0
'Apricot Nectar' 8.0
'Charisma' 8.0
'Cherish' 8.0
'Deep Purple' 8.0
'Eye Paint' 8.0
'Ginger' 8.0
'Gingersnap' 8.2
'Marina' 8.0
'Orangeade' 8.0
'Rose Parade' 8.0
'Sarabande' 8.0
'Sunsprite' 8.0
'Traumerei' 8.0
'Trumpeter' 8.0

Grandifloras
'Pink Parfait' 8.9
'Queen Elizabeth' 8.9
'Sonia' 8.2
'Ole' 8.2

A mass planting of pink floribunda roses on either side of a red brick path makes for a welcome sight.

William Warriner, Rose Hybridizer

Viewed from the bird's-eye vantage of a helicopter, the scene would look incongruous. On one side of a high dirt embankment, a group of men busily engaged in small arms practice; on the other, a solitary figure standing among thousands of multi-hued roses.

The roses and rifles are neighbors—a rifle range and a rose garden nestled against the softly rolling backdrop of the Santa Ana mountains in California. Both are a tiny part of the more than 80,000 acres that comprise the giant Irvine Ranch. The rifles are in the hands of marines from nearby El Toro Marine Air Base. The roses are in the hands of William Warriner, director of plant research for the world's largest rose growers, Jackson & Perkins, who maintain research facilities on almost six Irvine acres. At a compact 165 pounds, Warriner looks more like the marine he was than the rose breeder he is today.

Warriner's office, adjacent to the greenhouses, has a picture view of the Santa Anas, across which cowboys still drive cattle to pasture. The office where he recently commented on his profession is spacious but spartan, a clue that its occupant is more at home outside it than in it.

"I suppose rose breeding sounds glamorous," he said. "It is interesting and creative, but it involves a lot of details, a lot of hard work, and a lot of disappointments. Four months a year it's a nose-to-the-grindstone, seven-day-a-week job because you only get a few chances to look at the new seedlings. And if you miss them," he grinned, "you blow it. The other eight months are spent in the fields, evaluating seedlings—looking at all those mistakes you made that first year." If Warriner made any mistakes "that first year," they aren't obvious.

Rose breeding is a long-range endeavor. Roses crossed this year and selected for introduction won't appear in American gardens until 1986 at least, possibly not until 1989. Warriner hybridized his first roses for Jackson & Perkins in 1963, the year he was named to head Jackson & Perkins' California research operations. One of them became 'Golden Gate', Jackson & Perkins' Rose of the Year; another became 'Medallion'—a 1973 All-America Rose Selection and Rose of the Year. Roses he hybridized in the sixties but has not yet introduced won four gold medals, two silver medals, and two certificates in European rose trials this past summer, plus one silver medal and two certificates in Japan.

An intense, decisive man (a helpful characteristic for a man who each year must select 6 or 8 future varieties from over 100,000 new seedlings), Warriner dropped out of college during World War II to enlist in the marines. He was in his junior year at Michigan State University. The period immediately follow-

An "official" portrait of Warriner's winners: Cherish, a shell pink floribunda; Love, a red and white grandiflora; and Honor, a white hybrid tea.

ing the war was spent in Japan, where his organizational talents were utilized in helping supervise the disarmament. Discharged a captain, he reentered Michigan State and received his Bachelor of Science degree in floriculture.

Warriner began his nursery career as a pot plant grower in Milford, Michigan, an occupation that ended abruptly when he became snowbound one morning going to work. By the time he was mobile again, he had decided to keep on moving—all the way to California.

Armed with his degree in floriculture, he walked into Howard and Smith Nursery and into his life's work; there are only a handful of professional rose breeders and Fred Howard was one of them. He developed many early AARS winners and in 1916, with the variety 'Los Angeles', was the first American to win the prestigious Bagatelle award at the Bagatelle Gardens in Paris. Under his tutelage, Warriner learned the intricacies of creating new roses.

In 1972 Warriner garnered a "first" of his own, being the first American to win a gold medal in the Class A category at rose trials in The Hague, Netherlands. The trials match hybrid teas against floribundas to determine the outstanding garden variety. Like Howard, he is also a Bagatelle winner.

In 1956 he opened his own nursery in the small central California city of Patterson, which he operated until 1963 when he accepted a position with Jackson & Perkins as California Director of Plant Research. After the death of Eugene Boerner in 1966 (Boerner was a long-time, world renown hybridizer at J&P), Warriner shouldered the company's entire research efforts.

Warriner initiated a major change in hybridizing systems in 1967. Under the former system, seedlings were potted and later lined out in the fields, where they were observed through 2 or 3 growth cycles. Under the new system, seeds are planted in raised greenhouse benches and initial varieties selected within 6 months. Warriner feels he gets as good an indication of a seedling's worth as with the previous method and saves up to 30 months' time.

"New roses," says Warriner, "are as eagerly awaited each year by the gardening public as new cars are anticipated by the driving public." He carried the automobile analogy a step further. "We may have an Edsel once in a while, but luckily these don't ever make it to the market."

The ones that are getting on the market are better. According to Warriner, "Improvement over the years is very slow, but it's there, although some roses are only slightly different and only for a short time. Our goal is to develop new and better roses, whether or not they fit any previously conceived categories, and some of our new roses don't fit the standard hybrid tea, floribunda, or grandiflora classifications."

In his current breeding program, Warriner is seeking more usable roses—plants with good habit, that bloom freely, are easy to grow, will thrive with a minimum of care, and will develop good blooms in all kinds of weather. "This may mean," he advises, "roses that are not fully double, as some people prefer, but ones that are colorful, useful and have good form. In the long run they'll be much improved over those that open only under best conditions and will be less trouble to the rosarian and more acceptable for use by people who have only a few roses and little or no experience in rose growing."

On the subject of amateur rose hybridizers, Warriner had these comments: "Being an amateur hybridizer must have some very satisfying rewards. Although I have always been paid to do this work, I might have taken it as a hobby had I chosen another field to earn a living by. Possessing something unique is a facet of many hobbies. Collectors of things place the highest of value on the rarest items.

"The rose breeder, amateur or professional, must guard against placing too high a value on his or her own seedlings just because they are unique and one's own. The nursery will soon become overcrowded with really useless unnamed varieties with nothing but sentimental value if all but the very best are not discarded quickly. From our rather large number of seedlings about 1,000 are selected each year for budding, but the second year evaluation reduces this number to only 20 or 30.

"It is always amazing how horrible some selections can look in the budded field when they were thought to be pretty good on the seedling bench. Some cannot even survive budding. When a budded seedling appears promising in the field, it is rebudded in larger quantities and transplanted to test gardens. Further evaluations reduce the number of selections but these are budded in much larger quantities. A budding of about 500 is necessary to have sufficient plants to enter A.A.R.S. trials. This must be followed up with thousands to provide enough budwood for all the member nurseries, should a variety win.

"I can think of no vocation that I would rather be a part of than commercial rose breeding. There are rarely any boring days at the office and never a wish that I worked at something else. Sure, there are times when it seems none of the seedlings are showing promise, but these are always interrupted by an especially good find. There are disappointments at not winning an AARS award with leading varieties but there are extra thrills when our contenders do well all over the world. I can't help but feel proud that two of the varieties from my work were chosen as models for the Special Issue of the fifteen cent stamp, 'Red Masterpiece' and 'Medallion'."

And for 1980, William Warriner has every reason to feel even prouder. For the first time in history, all three All-America Rose Selection categories have been captured by roses from the same hybridizer—namely Warriner. Chosen for 1980 were 'Love' (grandiflora), 'Honor' (hybrid tea) and 'Cherish' (floribunda). The catalog descriptions of the award-winning roses read this way:

'Love': "A distinctive addition to the grandiflora class—and a colorful asset to the rose garden. Heavily petaled blooms are bicolor, with bright red petals reversing to silvery white. Once in bloom, flower production never stops. Abundant, striking flowers are ideally distributed over the full, stately bush. It looks absolutely great all season long, yet demands no special attention. It has pleased judges in rose trials at Monza, Rome, Madrid, and Japan, and here in America it is among the most consistent performers available to the rose gardener today."

'Honor': "In a year of exceptionally fine roses, it takes an especially fine rose to stand out, and this is that rose. This incomparable white hybrid tea has won six additional awards from all over the world, including the All America Selection here at home. Few white roses can match its bloom production and near-weatherproof habit. Pointed 1- to 1½-inch buds open beautifully in all weathers to satiny 4- to 5-inch blooms of brilliant pure white. Many are borne singly, and even in clusters their stems are of good cutting length, with few thorns.

William Warriner inside one of the greenhouses where breeding work is done in Tustin, California.

The growing of standards, or tree roses, takes extra time and skill—hence their increased cost.

The bush is vigorous, very mildew resistant, with upright habit and medium height. New canes 'break' effortlessly from the base, making a full, well-branched plant."

'Cherish': "An early bloomer that goes all out, all season long. Perfect, high-pointed buds are carried in profusion of a wide, well-leafed plant. The appealing flowers, colored a soft shell pink, are larger than most floribundas—about 4 inches across. They are beautifully set off by dark green, glossy foliage. Cut for arrangements, the blooms last very well, and have a slight but pleasing fragrance. This is a most vigorous rose, with unbeatable flower production and extremely attractive blooms. In addition to the All-America Selection, 'Cherish' has also won the Silver Medal at the Bagatelle rose trials in France."

Roses Of Yesterday And Today

In a small mountain canyon near Watsonville, California there is a small nursery that specializes in old, rare, and unusual roses. The canyon is dense with great redwoods, maples, and ferns, and the scene is complimented by a rippling stream. It is a unique spot for a unique nursery, one that has captured the imagination and loyalty of a growing group of gardeners since 1932. At that time the nursery was known as The Lester Rose Garden. It was a small nursery —shipping perhaps 4,500 plants a year—primarily known for its selection of rare native plants.

When Mr. Lester died, his widow entered into a partnership with Will Tillotson and the nursery became known as Lester & Tillotson's. Will Tillotson had been in the orange shipping business in southern California before retiring to northern California. His garden of old and rare roses in Redlands, California was well-known to admirers of old roses across the nation. In 1952 Will Tillotson became the sole owner of the nursery and the name changed once again to Will Tillotson's Roses of Yesterday and Today. During his ownership, Tillotson greatly expanded the availability of old roses by traveling extensively through Europe and sending specimens back to the United States. Even then, the procedure was complicated by the fact that all plant material had to be sent to either Ohio or Iowa State University (two universities that had permits from the United States Department of Agriculture to do this type of growing) for a 2-year quarantine period.

Will Tillotson died in England in 1957 and the business passed to his assistant, Dorothy Stemler. In the 1980 catalog Dorothy Stemler's daughter, Patricia Stemler Wiley, writes: "Dorothy Stemler, my mother, affectionately called 'The Lady of Old Roses,' wrote 19 catalogs and worked lovingly with the roses and the business until her death in 1976. Over the years of working alongside her in the office and growing fields, I absorbed much of her vast knowledge. I am continually amazed at the 'storehouse' she gave me to draw upon in answering your questions, or in handling everyday matters in business.

"In the last years of her life, mother had the desire to simplify the name 'Tillotson's Roses of Yesterday and Today' by just dropping the 'Tillotson's'. She and I agreed this would be done when I found the time expedient. When the business had to be re-registered in my name, I found it was a good time to make the change."

Patricia Wiley continues to expand the nursery's selection of old and rare roses. From the time a "new" old variety is imported, it takes approximately 7 years before it appears in the catalog. The process goes something like this: 10 to 12 pieces of budwood from the new variety are shipped to the United

The late Dorothy Stemler and her daughter, Patricia Stemler Wiley, stand in the garden of old roses near their nursery.

States, where they are coordinated with a rootstock and budded in late spring. The plants are all grown in one registered location and the USDA regularly inspects the variety for any sign of disease for a period of 2 years. If any problem is discovered, the plants are immediately destroyed. After the 2-year quarantine period is over, the USDA okays their release and the plants are dug up and sent to various trial gardens in the United States. For the next 2 years or so, notes are kept concerning the plant's performance and budwood is collected. The variety is not listed in the catalog until 200 #1 grades are available (see page 37).

There are 228 varieties listed in the 1980 catalog, with another 20 on their way. Patricia Wiley says that there are literally thousands of "undiscovered" old rose varieties still in existence, primarily in Europe, just waiting to be identified. The identification of these roses is not a simple process, and it is severely hampered by the fact that there are so few people who have the necessary expertise to do the job. Nevertheless, every year a few new varieties make their way into the catalog, making it an eagerly awaited publication for many rose gardeners.

The offices, rose storage shed, packing shed, and display garden are all in the mountain canyon location, but the actual growing of the stock takes place in

A beautiful combination of old roses: Harrison's Yellow and Alchymist.

Common moss rose

Crested moss rose

Empress Josephine

Comtessa de Murinais

Eglantine

Lavender Lassie

Madame Alfred Carriere

La Reine Victoria

Celsiana

Salet

Gloire des Mousseux

Madame Hardy

MacFarland, a small town in California's great central valley. Owing to its proximity to the coast, winters in Watsonville are very mild and roses grown there never really get the chance to go completely dormant. The central valley has winters cold enough to ensure that the bushes enter dormancy so that they can be shipped safely.

In the catalog, Patricia Wiley addresses the frequently asked question: "Will roses grown in the mild climate of California be hardy in severe climates?" She answers by saying: "Hardiness is inherent in the rose variety, and the best plants are those grown under ideal conditions. California's long months of sun and growing weather, enough frost in the fall to allow the plants to become naturally dormant, and controlled irrigation, are perfect conditions for producing the finest rose plants. The majority of roses you purchase for spring planting are grown on the West Coast, no matter where you buy them.

"California's long growing season makes it impossible to ship California grown roses for fall planting. Many of them are in bloom in October and do not start to go dormant until some time in November. We strongly recommend that California-grown roses be spring planted."

All the roses are shipped bare root, and are moderately priced considering their uniqueness. For the most part, care of the old roses is similar to their modern counterparts, with the exception of pruning. Mrs. Wiley writes: "Books and newspaper and magazine articles are published many times each year covering all phases of cultivation and care of roses. Planting and care of modern, shrub, old and species roses are the same, except for pruning . . . and it makes all the difference.

"As a general rule, prune roses that bloom repeatedly in the late winter or early spring before new growth starts. Prune the once-annual flowering roses only *after* they have bloomed in the spring.

"Study your roses so that you begin to know their personalities. Some of the

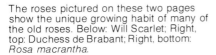

The roses pictured on these two pages show the unique growing habit of many of the old roses. Below: Will Scarlet; Right, top: Duchess de Brabant; Right, bottom: *Rosa macrantha.*

older varieties that bloom repeatedly should not be pruned except to remove weak or dead growth . . . their beauty is in a large plant with hundreds of flowers, and if you prune them like a hybrid tea or a floribunda you will not get a mass of bloom.

"To create a bushy, many branched plant, shorten the long canes by ⅓ *after the plant blooms*, and shorten lateral canes a few inches. If you wish, keep this up until late summer, then leave the plant alone until *after it blooms* the next spring.

"Pegging is the use of any method to bring the canes into an arched or horizontal position. It may be done by hooking about an 8-gauge wire over a matured cane and securing it in the desired position by pushing the other end of the wire into the ground, or by tying the canes in an arched position to stakes. This causes flowering stems to grow all along the canes. Just 2 or 3 canes arched over and tied to stakes will make it possible to weave other canes among them for a delightful effect. Fastening the long canes to fencing is effective.

"After about 2 years it is a good idea to remove a few old canes as new ones grow from the base of the plant."

The nursery expects to ship some 35 to 40 thousand roses this year. When asked if the number of orders increase each year Patricia Wiley exclaimed: "I don't know where all the people are coming from who want to grow old roses." She surmises that the current trend in things historical, preservation of the past, and even tracing one's family roots have all contributed to the interest in old roses. She also noted that many people have given her descriptions of their older homes—whether colonial, Victorian, or Mediterranean—asking for variety suggestions appropriate for the surrounding garden. For Patricia Wiley, it is extremely gratifying to see these historically accurate gardens being created. Not only does it ensure the survival of certain varieties, but the increased interest means support to rescue more old varieties from obscurity.

If you are interested in knowing more about old roses, you can request the catalog by writing: Roses of Yesterday and Today, 802 Brown's Valley Road, Watsonville, California 95076. There is a $1.00 charge for the catalog.

Note: When asked to select some of her favorite old rose varieties, Patricia Wiley responded by sending portraits of the roses that appear on page 101 and here.

CUT ROSES

Whether you choose one lovely bloom in a bud vase or a basket of mixed varieties, roses can add beauty, color, and fragrance to your interior environment.

Legend has it that Cleopatra once filled a room knee-deep with roses to welcome Marc Anthony. We know that the Romans imported shiploads of roses to make garlands and bouquets for festive occasions. And Nero once lavished so many roses on his banquet guests that several people suffocated underneath the great piles of petals.

Today, you can enjoy cut roses 12 months a year—in season, your own garden flowers; any time, commercially grown blooms.

When you cut roses from the garden, choose blooms that are only partly opened. Studies indicate that flowers cut in the late afternoon last longest. Don't cut more stem and foliage than you need—plants need abundant leaf supply to stay productive.

It's a good idea to carry a bucket of water with you to the garden.

Cut the rose at an angle with a sharp knife or shears, and place it immediately in the water. Cut at a point where a 5-leaflet leaf appears on the stem (see pruning, page 49). Allow at least 2 leaves to remain between the cut and the main stem. When you've finished gathering the bouquet, wash away any soil or leaf spray residue from the foliage.

Whether your cut roses come from the garden or the florist, if you follow these tips you will increase their life span. It may be tempting to place them in a vase to enjoy immediately; but if you take the time to prepare your roses properly, they'll last much longer.

Remove all thorns and foliage that will be below the water level in your vase. This will keep the water sweet smelling and free of most bacteria.

The easy way to remove foliage is to take several layers of paper towel or cloth, wrap them around the stem where you wish to begin removal, and pull downward to the end of the stem, stripping away thorns and leaves as you pull. Never scrape the stem with a knife—the resulting injuries will shorten the life of the flowers. If the rose has only a few leaves and thorns, simply break them off with your fingers. But be careful—rose thorns can hurt.

Give the rose a fresh cut at least 1/2 inch above the end of the stem. Cut with a sharp knife at a sharp angle in order to expose as much cut surface to the water as possible.

Immerse the stems in deep water that is too hot for your hand (about 90° to 100°F.). Leave the roses alone until the water cools, then place the entire container in the refrigerator or a cool place for a couple of hours to condition the blooms. (You usually can revive wilted roses by giving them a fresh cut and subjecting them to this hot sauna treatment.)

When you are ready to arrange the flowers, fill a vase with fresh water and add a floral preservative (from flower shops or garden stores), carefully following manufacturer's directions. Too much preservative will put the roses into irrevocable shock.

Arrange the flowers any way you like, giving each one a fresh slanted cut before you place it. Keep the finished bouquet in as cool a place as possible,

away from drafts. Add enough fresh water daily to keep the stems immersed to 1/2 or 2/3 of their length. Better yet, change the water every day, adding new preservative each time. The flowers will last even longer if you recut the bottom of the stem every day or so.

If you plan to use florist's foam for arranging, prepare a solution of fresh water and floral preservative, and soak the foam thoroughly in this solution. Once you have placed the stem in the foam do not move it, or air pockets will form at the base of the stem, cutting off the water supply. Keep the container filled with plenty of fresh water.

In addition to beautifying the interior environment, flowers gently remind us of our link with all living things. They offer us a quiet, inner celebration of nature. Cut blooms add tranquility to any room. Live plants are dependent upon light for survival, but we can enjoy colorful cut roses even in the dimmest corners.

The arrangement of flowers is a very personal thing. Some people prefer to adhere to the strict rules of floral design that came into being with the American garden clubs, the principles followed in the arrangement category at rose shows. Others prefer English-type mixed flower baskets, the simple Oriental touch, or just a lone specimen rose in a bud vase.

Nowadays, the trend is toward more natural bouquets, letting the flowers speak for themselves without imposing rigid lines or contrived forms on them. In any case, don't just imitate—create, and express your own personal feelings for the roses.

Choose containers that fit the mood of the room or the occasion. Select a vase that visually relates in size with the blooms. Gleaming silver or other metal reflects the beauty of roses. Wicker baskets are good choices for garden-fresh casual bouquets, while china, porcelain, or ceramic containers are best suited to more formal arrangements. Clear glass or crystal allows you to enjoy the entire rose from the stem up. This look is most successful if mechanical holders and florist's foam are not used.

Roses are beautiful alone or with several varieties mixed together. They blend successfully with other garden flowers, as well. Nothing beats rose foliage for greens, but you might try using camellia, ivy, or rose-scented geranium leaves for additional interest.

Above: Ways to prolong the life of cut roses (page 106).
Right: The magic of candlelight flickering on a single red rose is captured by our photographer. The bloom floats atop a leaf of rose-scented geranium in a silver bowl.

Above left: Tiny miniature roses in a jam
jar complement an afternoon tea tray.
Above right: A classical rose arrangement
—long-stemmed roses simply displayed
in a clear crystal cylinder. Left: Three tiny
Tiffany crystal bottles show off blooms
of miniatures June Time, Fire Princess,
and Lavender Lace.

Showing Prize Roses

Growing prize-winning blooms is a skillful art that requires continual practice. A lot of work and a good bit of luck are needed to grow a rose that reaches its most beautiful phase just in time for a rose show. It takes preparation well in advance, disbudding at just the right time to create large flowers, and extra protection from the elements, insects, and diseases. See pages 46-47 for pruning methods used to produce exhibition-quality roses.

Rose shows begin at the local level. Then come the district shows, then two annual national competitions sponsored by the American Rose Society. Check your local newspaper gardening news or calendar of events for nearby shows. Or write to the ARS for complete information on rose shows. (See page 136 for address.)

Competition is steep. Judging is based on a point system: Color—25, Form—25, Substance—20, Stem and foliage—20, and Size—10. All judges must be trained and accredited by the ARS. Winners in various categories are awarded ribbons, certificates, medals, trophies, and other appropriate prizes.

Whether you want to grow exhibition roses for competition or for your own enjoyment, you can learn a lot from studying the entries and winners at a rose show. No matter what stage of the competition, any rose show is a great place for the amateur and expert alike to actually see what the flowers of hundreds of varieties actually look like up close. For the person just getting interested in growing roses, a show is the perfect opportunity to pick what varieties he or she likes best and perhaps talk to the growers about their cultural methods.

Busy hands groom the specimen blooms that will soon be displayed, first for the judges, then for the public.

Above: Blooms are displayed together by classification. Identification tags are folded to hide entrant's name until after the judging. Below: Winning roses are displayed in a special area along with their prizes.

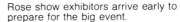

Far right: A living room "rose show" featuring all the varieties from the garden grouped together in a collection of glass cylinders.

Rose show exhibitors arrive early to prepare for the big event.

PRESERVING ROSES

Here are some old-fashioned ways, and maybe, even a few new ones, to preserve your flowers or hips in the form of decorative accessories, fragrances and cosmetics.

According to mythology, when the gods created the rose they showered it with gifts. Dionysius, for example, bestowed nectar and fragrance on the flower. Later, the pharaohs of Egypt supervised the bottling of this fragrance, creating the first rose potpourri.

The Romans, in typical excessive fashion, stuffed themselves on delicacies made of rose petals, and rose wine flowed freely.

When a Persian caliph discovered roses floating on petal-strewn waters, he interrupted his wedding festivities to bottle some of their oil; thus was born one of Persia's major industries. When the Arabs conquered Persia they became enamored of roses, and rose water became a major flavoring in Arabian cookery.

American colonial women turned rose petals into a plastic substance and fashioned it into jewelry.

There is really nothing new or strange about the desire to continue enjoying roses after the gardening season has passed. Perhaps it's because you're sentimental. Or maybe you just hate to waste anything, and enjoy finding ways to use everything. Whatever your reason, you can keep enjoying your beautiful roses long after the flowers in the garden have faded into memory.

Preserving roses is fun for the family, and the dried flowers, fragrances, soaps, oils, and other rose creations make delightful gifts for friends with whom you'd like to share part of your garden.

Dry Roses For Lasting Beauty

If you've never dried roses before, you'll find that not only is it easy to do but in addition it's highly rewarding because of the lasting pleasure the flowers provide. You can dry one or two roses or many of them for bouquets or arrangements. And the relatively low cost also will add to your enjoyment.

One easy way is simply to tie the rose stems together and hang them upside down in a warm dry place. If there's a lot of dust, wrap them gently in cheesecloth. Unfortunately, most of the color is lost with this method.

You can get better results by completely immersing the flowers in a desiccant, which gradually withdraws all the moisture from them. Small rosebuds or blooms with only a few petals dry most successfully. The flowers will last indefinitely; you can use them in winter bouquets and holiday decorations over and over again.

Reds and other deep colors will darken; pinks and yellows will fade slightly, although some light-colored blooms will retain much of their natural color for several seasons.

Gather roses in the morning, after the dew has dried. Cut off the stems and insert a short piece of florist's wire through the heel of the rose.

Types of desiccants. Craft or hobby stores as well as garden centers sell several commercial preparations for drying flowers. However, the following drugstore or hardware materials seem to work equally well: household borax pow-

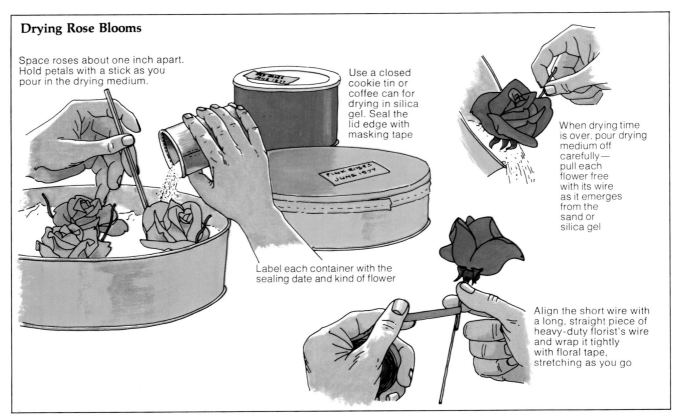

Drying Rose Blooms

Space roses about one inch apart. Hold petals with a stick as you pour in the drying medium.

Use a closed cookie tin or coffee can for drying in silica gel. Seal the lid edge with masking tape

When drying time is over, pour drying medium off carefully—pull each flower free with its wire as it emerges from the sand or silica gel

Label each container with the sealing date and kind of flower

Align the short wire with a long, straight piece of heavy-duty florist's wire and wrap it tightly with floral tape, stretching as you go

der; oven-dried, fine-grained builder's sand (or beach sand washed in a bucket of detergent and rinsed several times); equal parts cornmeal and household borax; ground or crushed silica gel crystals (originally, these are blue, but moisture turns them white. Between uses, spread them on a cookie sheet and dry them in a low-temperature oven until the white crystals return to their original blue).

Method. Select an airtight container such as a large coffee can or plastic food storage box. Pour a layer of the chosen desiccant over the bottom of the container. Place the flower upright on top and bend the wire flat. Use the fingers of one hand to hold the bottom of the flower, while with the other hand you slowly add more desiccant around the rose.

Be sure to work the material in between and completely around *every* petal. Air pockets can invite mildew. Use a small artist's paintbrush to push lightweight materials such as borax into cavities. All this takes some time; you'll need a little patience.

Add as many flowers as the container will hold, as long as none of the blooms touch each other. After the last flower is in place, cover with 2 more inches of the desiccant material. If using sand, leave the container uncovered. For all other materials, seal tightly. Use tape to hold the lid in place if it isn't airtight.

Carefully place the container in a warm dry area where it can remain undisturbed until the roses are dried. Most blooms in borax or silica gel require 2 to 3 days. In sand they will take 1 to 3 weeks.

If you don't have a warm dry place to store the container, or if you're in a hurry, place the container in an unlighted gas oven. The pilot light will keep it warm and dry; or use an electric warming oven at 150°F. If you choose oven drying, be sure to use metal containers. You don't have to seal the container. Sand will dry the blooms in a few days; silica gel or borax will dry them in about 10 to 15 hours. However, if you use the fast method you will lose some of the blooms' color clarity.

To test readiness using any of these methods, gently remove a flower from the container. It should feel dry and crisp and make a rustling sound when you touch it. If it is not completely dry, return it to the box and cover it completely, once again. Test the following day (or in a few hours, if using the oven method).

When the flowers are dry, carefully remove them from the container, hold them upside down, and gently shake off the desiccant. Use your small brush to remove any material that clings to the bloom.

Store the dried flowers in a dry room away from direct sunlight until you are ready to use them. To make stems longer, add any desired length of florist's wire and wrap with florist tape, stretching it as you go.

Hips For Winter Decoration

Colorful clusters of rose-hip fruits are attractive in arrangements, as package decorations, on holiday trees or wreaths, and for other imaginative uses. Their bright color will fade slightly to deep orange when dried in the following manner.

Fresh rose hips are gathered when they reach brilliant color. They may be turned into delicious syrups or jams, or dried for later use.

Mix 1 part glycerin (from your pharmacy) to 2 parts very hot water in a tightly closed bottle. Shake well to mix thoroughly. Pour into a saucepan and bring to boiling point.

Place clusters of rose hips in a container, stem up, and pour in the glycerin mixture so the solution will reach about 2 inches up the stems.

Normally, it takes 2 to 3 weeks for rose hips to become preserved. Once every part of the plant material has absorbed the water and glycerin, the hips should be soft and shiny. The water evaporates and leaves the glycerin behind in the cells, preserving the hips indefinitely.

Check regularly to see that the hips do not absorb all the solution before preservation is complete. If the solution is gone, pour in more hot water (not boiling, this time) up to the original level.

If beads of moisture appear on the surface of the fruit, then the hips have been in solution longer than necessary and cannot absorb any more. Remove them from the solution and wipe off the excess moisture.

Before storing or using the preserved hips, spray them lightly with hair lacquer. Keep them in a cool dry room to retain suppleness.

Pressed Petals And Leaves

Almost everyone remembers pressing flowers as a school science project. You placed the blooms between sheets of newsprint or blotting paper, inserted the sheets between pages of a large heavy book, and weighted them down with several other books until the petals dried.

Well, for those of you who want to keep a few of the petals and leaves from your roses to turn into pictures, notecards, or other personal remembrances, here's a slightly more sophisticated method of utilizing a flower press.

You can buy a flower press in a hobby or toy store, but it's more fun to make your own. Simply cut two 1-foot squares of plywood. Drill holes 1 inch from each corner. Cut several pieces of corrugated cardboard and sheets of blotting paper to fit inside, cutting off the corners to allow room for screws to pass.

Stack layers of cardboard, blotting paper, petals or leaves, more blotting paper, and cardboard. Continue alternating layers until the press is filled (make sure the petals are not touching when you lay them on the blotting paper).

Insert 3- to 4-inch screws and fasten tightly with wing nuts (see diagram on page 116). Store the press in a warm dry place for at least 4 weeks. The longer the petals are pressed initially, the better they will retain color.

When you are ready to use the flowers, unscrew the press, remove the sheets, and lift off the petals and leaves carefully with tweezers. If you must keep them for a while before making a design, store them between tissue sheets in envelopes in a warm dry place to keep them from absorbing moisture.

Press many kinds of flowers and leaves so you'll have a good selection for your creations.

To decorate cards, first form your design. Then glue the petals down with thinned rubber cement. Burnish by covering with tissue paper and rubbing the

Pressing Petals and Leaves

You'll need 2 pieces of plywood, 6 sheets of corrugated cardboard, 10 pieces of blotter paper, and 4 stove bolts ¼" x 3" with washers and wing nuts, along with your petals and leaves.

Place petals and leaves on blotter so they don't touch. Cover with another blotter

Handle dried petals by grasping well toward the center with tweezers—edges are very delicate

Stack each pair of blotters between cardboard and the whole stack between plywood—tighten wing nuts

surface with your fingers or a flat stick. When the glue dries, carefully rub off the excess from around the edges of the petals.

If you want to create a picture with your flowers and leaves, select a suitable piece of artist's mounting board. Cut this to the size you wish and lay the plant material down to form a design. Then carefully glue each piece to the board with rubber cement, as you would in making cards.

When the picture is complete, wrap it temporarily in blotting paper until it's time to frame it.

Place the picture flush to the glass of the frame; this will make it as airtight as possible and prevent deterioration. Add a piece of heavy cardboard to the back and seal it to the frame with masking tape.

For a more contemporary design, glue the petals directly onto a piece of glass or lucite, cover with a duplicate sheet of glass or lucite, and clip together. These "frames" are available in many good frame shops.

To retain good color, hang your flower pictures as far away from direct sunlight as possible.

Capturing The Fragrance Of The Rose In Potpourri, Candles, Soaps, And Beads

"The rose looks fair, but fairer it we deem for that sweet odor which doth in it live." When Shakespeare wrote these words he must have had potpourri (pō poo reé) in mind. This pleasant old way to preserve the memory of a lovely rose garden still delights today as it has for centuries.

The custom probably originated with the pharaohs, who buried pots of roses for years. The French called the concoction "rotten pot" because in the old moist method of making potpourri, petals actually rotted slowly in a jar. The jar was opened to relieve the stale atmosphere of damp stuffy houses.

Today, the dry method usually is used to make potpourri; but no matter how it's produced it can still sweeten the air with its heady aroma. Use your imagination for ways of packaging the fragrant mixture to create unique gifts. Potpourri is a sentimental way to share the beauty and fragrance of your roses with friends.

Creating Potpourri

Pick roses in the early morning, after the dew has gone. The fresher the flower, the more essential oil will remain when it is dried. As to varieties, let your nose be the judge in choosing fragrances.

Cut the flowers and gently pull off the petals. Dry a few small leaves and some tiny buds each time. Dry other fragrant garden flowers (lavender, violets, freesia), leaves, and herbs at the same time and in the same way, to mix with the roses.

Select an area away from strong light, where warm air can circulate. Spread the petals, leaves, and buds on some sort of drying rack, such as a window screen, or on cheesecloth or newspaper on a tabletop or the floor. If the area is breezy, put a layer of cheesecloth over the petals. Stir or turn them daily.

For moist potpourri, dry the petals for only a few days—just until they are limp, not crisp. Flowers going into dry mixtures, however, should be completely dried to the crisp stage (like cereal flakes). This usually takes from 4 days to 2 weeks, depending on the moisture in the petals and in the air.

If you are in a hurry, spread the petals on a cookie sheet and place them in a warm oven (110°F.). Leave the door open to allow moisture to escape. Stir gently or shake the sheets from time to time so the petals will dry evenly. Drying usually takes 1 to 2 hours. Then the flowers are ready to be turned into potpourri, according to one of the recipes below or your own creation.

You'll need to mix the petals with fixatives, which will absorb the fragrant oils and preserve the fragrance. Common fixatives include orrisroot, benzoin or storax, calamus powder, violet powder, ambergris, and gum storax. A quarter pound of any one of these is enough for a 1-quart potpourri.

To make *dry* potpourri, mix the petals with the fixative and add whatever spices and other fragrant materials you wish. Mix well and store in a covered container for several weeks, until the fragrances blend and mellow. Then place the mixture in several containers with removable lids. If you use clear glass, you will have the extra pleasure of seeing the contents' pretty colors. Or you can sew the mixture inside little bags or pillows (sachets) to store inside drawers or closets to keep them sweet smelling. You also can keep potpourri in open baskets of wicker or silver, but you'll need to wrap it in a piece of nylon net and tie it with a tiny ribbon to keep the petals and spices from spilling away.

Moist potpourris are heavier in fragrance and last longer than the dry type. Salt the slightly dried petals down in a crock, as in making pickles, with non-iodized salt mixed with spices, fragrant oils, and a bit of brandy or perfume. Stir the mix daily for about a month until the scents are well blended and mellowed. It is a good idea to weight the petals down while they are mellowing to draw all the oils out from them. If any broth forms, mix it in with the petals.

When the blend is mellow, pour it into a large container and mix well once again. Place in small porcelain, silver, or opaque glass containers with remov-

Far left: Old-fashioned potpourri containers.
Left: A sewing basket full of sachet notions.

able lids that you can open whenever you wish to fill the room with a summery aroma. At one time, it was easy to find "rose jars" with double lids—one solid, outer, removable lid and another inner lid with holes to let the fragrance escape. Today, you can buy such jars in some oriental art shops.

Whenever moist potpourri seems to be dry and losing its fragrance, pour a small amount of good-quality brandy over the top and mix in to reactivate the fragrant oils. Or moisten the mixture with a homemade rose scent, which you can make by placing rose petals in a bottle of wine or spirits. Cork the bottle tightly for 3 months—then open, add to the potpourri, and enjoy your roses once again.

Moist Potpourri

It is said that this old recipe will keep its fragrance for up to 50 years.

1 quart partially dried rose petals	¾ cup bay salt (recipe below)
2 cups mixed, partially dried, fragrant garden flowers (jasmine, orange blossoms, lavender, violets)	¼ cup crushed allspice
	¼ cup mashed cloves
	¼ cup brown sugar
	1 tablespoon crushed orrisroot
1 cup dried fragrant leaves	2 tablespoons brandy

1. Mix together the bay salt, allspice, cloves, and sugar.

2. Blend the flower petals and leaves with orrisroot. Place some of the petal mixture in a large crock and sprinkle with the salt mixture. Continue alternating layers of petals and salt.

3. Add the brandy. Cap tightly.

4. Open every day and stir.

5. After a month, pour into a large bowl and mix thoroughly. Fill small containers.

Bay Salt

3 broken bay leaves	1 cup noniodized salt

1. Pour salt over the bay leaves and crush with a wooden mallet or spoon, or with mortar and pestle, until the leaves are ground into tiny flakes.

Capture a rainbow of garden fragrances in oils and other scents and make your own herb and rose scented soaps or choose from a wide range of ready-made ones.

Jackson and Perkins Damp Sachet

1 quart partially dried rose petals
Approximately ¾ cup noniodized salt
1 ounce orrisroot or violet
   powder
Selected crushed spices and herbs
Vanilla beans, broken in small
   pieces
Perfume, cologne, or vinegar

1. After the rose petals have dried for 3 days, pack them in jars between layers of salt, adding to each layer sprinklings of orrisroot or violet powder. If desired, also add sprinklings of spices, herb seeds (such as caraway or cardamom), herb leaves (such as thyme, sweet marjoram, sage, mint, or rosemary), and broken vanilla beans.

2. Sprinkle the contents of a full jar with scent, cologne, or vinegar.

Note: You can add fragrant oils, powders, leaves, or blossoms of many types to make an even better damp-sachet potpourri. A more costly but more long-lasting potpourri of this type may be obtained by adding rose, jasmine, bergamot, lavender, or violet oils.

Caution: Again, prevent mold. Use enough salt to preserve.

American Rose Society's Old-Fashioned Rose Jar

Dried rose petals
Ground cloves, mace, and cinnamon
Perfume
Fragrant oils such as cedar,
   sandalwood, jasmine, heliotrope,
   violet, or lavender

1. Place a layer of dried petals in a jar with a tight-fitting lid. Sprinkle lightly with ground cloves, mace, and cinnamon.

2. Add another layer of petals and another of spices, alternating until you reach the top.

3. Add 5 to 10 drops of oil or extract. On the top sprinkle a few drops of your favorite perfume.

Note: If your garden boasts a variety of blooming plants and herbs, you can mix in dried blooms or leaves of lavender, rose geranium, lemon verbena, thyme, or heliotrope with the rose petals. Your rose jar will thus become a potpourri—more interesting to look at and wonderful to smell.

A still life arrangement of sachet and potpourri ingredients—all from the garden.

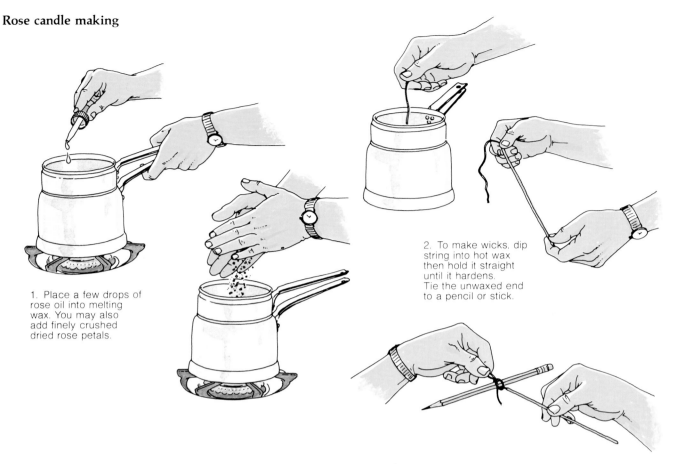

1. Place a few drops of rose oil into melting wax. You may also add finely crushed dried rose petals.

2. To make wicks, dip string into hot wax then hold it straight until it hardens. Tie the unwaxed end to a pencil or stick.

Jackson and Perkins Dry Sachet

1 quart dried rose petals
1 ounce orrisroot

½ teaspoon *each* cinnamon, ground cloves, allspice, mace, and sandalwood powder

1. Blend petals with orrisroot.

2. Make a mixture of cinnamon, ground cloves, allspice, mace, and sandalwood powder.

3. Place a layer of petals in a rose jar and sprinkle with some of the mixture. Repeat the process until the jar is full.

4. Close the jar tightly and store it until all the fragrances have mingled.

Caution: Moldy rose petals ruin the brew. If you're using the dry-sachet method, make sure all the petals are *totally* dry.

San Francisco Potpourri

4 cups dried rose petals and small buds
1 cup dried rose leaves
1 cup dried rose geranium leaves
1 tablespoon crushed benzoin
2 tablespoons dried citrus peel
1 tablespoon whole cloves, crushed
1 tablespoon whole allspice
1 teaspoon anise seed, crushed

1 tablespoon cardamom seed, crushed
1 whole nutmeg, crushed
2 bay leaves, finely broken
4 cinnamon sticks, broken into 1-inch pieces
Several drops *each* oils of patchouli, jasmine, rose geranium, and tuberose

1. Place rose petals and leaves, along with geranium leaves, in a large container. Sprinkle with benzoin.

2. Add the spices and mix together gently with your hands.

3. Spoon into selected containers and sprinkle oils on top. Close tightly for about 6 weeks, until the mixture is well aged.

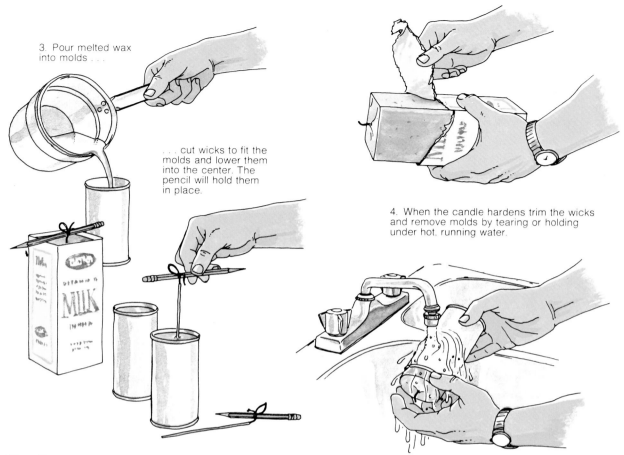

3. Pour melted wax into molds . . .

. . . cut wicks to fit the molds and lower them into the center. The pencil will hold them in place.

4. When the candle hardens trim the wicks and remove molds by tearing or holding under hot, running water.

Candles

Since both roses and candles are the essence of romance, what better combination could you have than a mixture of the two?

Paraffin wax blocks or pieces of leftover unscented candles
White string
Rose oil

Food coloring or pieces of wax crayons (optional)
Dried rose petals (optional)

1. Melt wax in a double boiler over low heat. Add a few drops of rose oil and finely crushed petals.

2. Cut string to fit length of mold, allowing a few extra inches. Dip in hot wax. Pull out and straighten to form wick. Tie unwaxed end to a pencil.

3. Pour hot wax into mold (see above). Lower wick into center of mold, holding in place with pencil resting across top of mold. One alternative is to pour the candle now and insert the wick later by sticking a heated icepick into the desired spot in the candle. Then simply put the wick into the hole left by the hot pick.

4. Allow to harden. Trim wick. Remove from mold.

Candle molds: You can get old-fashioned candle molds from craft shops. Or use pâté molds, clean milk cartons, any heavy-duty food container, or clean tin cans. Or make a round mold from heavy-duty cardboard cylinders and secure a thick cardboard bottom with masking tape to form an airtight mold. For floating candles, use shallow, individual salad molds. Once the candles are hard, you can simply tear away the cardboard molds. Remove candles from metal molds by running a little hot water over the outside until the candle slips out.

Rose Soaps

Whether you enjoy taking a brisk shower or soaking in a hot tub, these soaps will make the experience a delight—almost like a walk in a summer rose garden.

The essence of fresh roses is an important ingredient in these homemade soaps, dusting powders, colognes, cold creams, and cleansers.

Old-Fashioned Rose-Scented Soap

10 pounds lard
Soft water
4 tablespoons sugar
2 tablespoons salt

6 tablespoons powdered borax
½ cup ammonia
1 gallon rose petals
Rose oil (optional)
2 cups lye

1. Outdoors, spread lard about 1 inch thick on a board. Use only roses that have never been treated with any type of pesticides (insecticides, fungicides, and so on), and push them deep into the lard. Cover with cheesecloth to protect from dust. Leave for 24 hours, then remove flowers. For stronger fragrance, add new blooms and leave another 24 hours.

2. After removing flowers, put lard in kettle with 2 quarts of water. Bring to boil. Cool overnight. Any foreign particles will sink to the bottom and can be scraped off the next morning.

3. Mix sugar, salt, powdered borax, and ammonia into 1 cup of water. Add a few drops of rose oil, if desired.

4. In outdoor area, mix 2 quarts cold water with 2 cups lye in a stainless steel or granite-ware pan. Closely follow all precautions and directions on lye label for preparation of lye.

5. Add the sugar, borax, and ammonia mixture.

6. Slowly add cool lard to lye mixture, stirring with a wooden spoon until thick and light in color.

7. Pour thickened soap into stainless steel or granite pan or a wooden box lined with a dampened cloth for easy removal.

8. Leave until soap is hard. The longer you let it dry, the longer each bar will last. Remove from mold and cut into desired portions.

9. Wrap in soft cloth saturated with rose oil to enhance the fragrance.

Soap from Leftovers

Scraps of unscented or glycerin soaps, cut into very fine pieces

Hot water (or hot rose water)
Rose oil

1. Pour hot water over soap shavings in a small saucepan. Add a few drops of oil. Place over low flame and stir until soap is dissolved.
2. Pour into molds and let harden.
3. To remove from metal molds, run a little warm water on outside of mold until soap slips out.

Molds: Use individual salad or pâté molds, or wash tin cans such as sardine or tuna cans. Cream or milk cartons (wash them first) can be torn away after the soap hardens. Then slice the soap into 1-inch-thick bars. Allow the soap to sit for a few days before using. This hardens it and makes it last longer.

Rose Beads For A Rosary Or For Jewelry

Rose beads are almost extinct nowadays. A few convents still make the beads from bridal roses so that the bride can keep part of her wedding bouquet. You may find this ancient art enjoyable. And the little beads will retain their fragrance for years.

Traditional Rose Beads

1 cup salt
1 cup rose petals, firmly packed

½ cup water
Oil paint (optional)

1. Heat salt and petals, mashing together. Stir in water and add paint for desired color, or leave natural for a brown bead.
2. Reheat, very low, over an asbestos pad, stirring constantly until smooth.
3. Roll out to ¼-inch thickness. Cut and roll beads in the palm of the hand to desired shape (oval, round, oblong) until they are smooth.
4. String the beads on florist's wire or waxed string fastened to a needle. Let beads dry in a dark place, moving them occasionally to keep them from sticking.
5. When dry, fashion into jewelry as desired. Wrap in a cloth saturated with rose perfume to increase fragrance.

Note: Should you prefer traditional black rosary beads, cook the petals with a rusty nail, or in a black iron pot with a piece of iron in it.

Bottling The Essence Of Roses

The rose is the most widely used flower of perfumers. Heavily fragrant damask roses of the exotic East are the kind used to extract attar of roses, an oil more costly than gold. It takes 10,000 pounds of petals to make one pound of attar of roses. No wonder those fine perfumes cost so much.

Perfumers obtain oils or pomades, as the solids are called, by steeping the rose petals in a mixture of lard and pure suet. The flowers give up their oils, since oil is attracted to oil.

Here's a simplified way of obtaining a little oil from your roses.

Extracting Rose Oil

Pour a quart of pure olive oil into a large mixing bowl or crock. Add as many fresh petals as the oil will take. Only use petals from plants that have not been treated with pesticides. Let soak for 1 or 2 days.

Then strain the oil through cheesecloth, mashing to squeeze all the oils from the wilted petals.

Once again, add as many fresh petals as the oil will take and let it set another day or so. Strain again. Repeat this process with at least 10 to 12 batches of petals. Then strain the oil a final time and pour into a bottle with a tight cap.

You can add this rose oil to all kinds of colognes, perfumes, cosmetics, potpourris, and other recipes in this section. Or you can simply wear the oil alone as a fragrance.

If you do not have enough flowers for this long procedure, you can buy rose oil from health-food stores, herbal cosmetic shops, old-fashioned drug stores, or suppliers of raw materials for perfumers in large cities.

Distilling Rose Nectar

Rose water has many uses. It is a major seasoning in Turkey, replacing catsup, salt, and pepper. In Egypt it's used as a beauty treatment as well as flavoring for candies, desserts, and drinks. In France it is an eyewash. It is the basis of numerous cosmetics and foods. To make many of the recipes in this section, you'll need to have rose water on hand.

Three methods of securing this nectar of the rose follow. If you haven't enough of either roses or time, you can purchase rose water from gourmet shops, especially those that carry Middle Eastern delicacies.

Select the most fragrant roses available. Only use petals from plants that have not been treated with pesticides. Remove petals and wash well. Cut off the bitter white tip from each petal if you plan to use rose water for cooking.

Method I—A simple laboratory still. Take 20 feet of copper tubing and roll it around a heavy cardboard tube to create a coil. Then mount that with copper wire to a simple 2″ by 4″ stand. (You can also purchase glass coils from scientific laboratory supply houses.) Attach rubber tubing to a large flask and a small beaker. (See photo.)

To operate, simply half-fill the flask with 2 quarts of water and 2 quarts of rose petals. (If you plan to use the rose water for fragrances rather than for food, then add 1 quart of pure alcohol instead of the water.)

Heat the petals and water slowly. You can use a hot plate or you can do it on

Method I — A simple laboratory still.

Method II—Stove-top Lab

Tea kettle of water and rose petals

Shallow pan of ice water

SUGAR SA

Rubber hose

Rose water drips into jar or bottle

the kitchen range. Place an asbestos pad under the flask, and keep the fire on a very low simmer.

Steam rises into the rubber tube and passes through the copper coils, where it cools. Then it goes into the receiver flask (which is wrapped in a damp towel), and rests in a pan of cool water. An electric fan helps speed up the condensation. Here the steam condenses into rose water.

Method II—Stove-top lab. Fill a regular tea kettle half full of water and cover the water thickly with rose petals. Attach a rubber hose to the spout and place the other end in a glass jar or bottle on the floor. Arrange the hose so that part of it is submerged in a pan of cold water en route to the jar. Simmer the kettle over low heat. This distillation principle is a simplified process of the preceding method.

Method III—Nondistillation. Use this method only for fragrances or cosmetics —not for cooking. Simply bring 2 quarts of distilled water to a boil. Remove from stove and add ⅛ ounce rose oil, 4 drops oil of clove, and 1 pint pure alcohol. Let stand several days before bottling.

Cosmetics And Colognes

Since antiquity, roses have been a major ingredient in cosmetic beauty preparations. Their popularity in cosmetology is mainly because of the fragrance they impart to moisturizers, skin fresheners, and cleansers. Psychologically, it feels clean and refreshing to rub your face with rose petals.

You can find all the ingredients used in the following cosmetics, colognes, and perfumes at old-fashioned drug stores, fancy pharmacies, herbal cosmetic shops, or from suppliers of raw materials for perfumers. Check your local yellow pages or ask your druggist for nearby sources.

"Alcohol" refers to 90 to 96 percent pure rectified alcohol. It costs more than the rubbing kind but it is odorless and colorless—as it must be for cosmetology.

Simple Rose Perfume

2 tablespoons rose oil   1¾ cups alcohol

1. Mix the oil and alcohol and pour into a clean bottle with a tight-fitting cap.
Note: You can create endless fragrances by adding varying amounts of other floral oils to the above.

Rose Cologne

4 tablespoons rose water   ⅓ cup spirit of jasmine
¼ teaspoon rose geranium oil   ¼ cup spirit of rose
1 tablespoon spirit of patchouli 1½ cups alcohol

1. Combine all ingredients and pour into a bottle or atomizer. Allow to set for at least 1 week before using.
Note: Add petals to a bottle of wine, brandy, or vodka for homemade floral spirits. Store for at least 3 months.

Rose Water and Glycerin

A famous, old, reliable twosome for facial cleansing.
1. Mix equal portions of glycerin (available from your pharmacist) with rose water.
2. Heat just to boiling and store in a capped bottle.

Rose Skin Freshener

¼ teaspoon camphor
1 teaspoon borax
1½ teaspoons tincture of benzoin

1 cup distilled water
½ cup rose water

1. Dissolve camphor and borax in benzoin.
2. Add water and rose water. Mix and bottle.

Rose Cleansing Milk

3 tablespoons pure soap flakes
3 tablespoons potassium carbonate
1½ cups hot water
2 tablespoons almond oil

8 drops rose oil
¼ cup alcohol
1 cup rose water

1. Dissolve soap flakes and potassium carbonate in water. Add almond oil. Cool.
2. Dissolve rose oil in alcohol. Add to first mixture.
3. Stir in rose water and pour into jars or bottles.

Rose Skin-Toning Lotion

½ teaspoon boric acid powder
4 teaspoons alcohol

2 tablespoons witch hazel
½ cup rose water

1. Dissolve boric acid in alcohol.
2. Add witch hazel and rose water. Let set for 1 week before using.

Rose Cold Cream

4 ounces almond oil
4 ounces rose water

1 ounce white wax

1. Pour almond oil in small saucepan and add wax. Melt slowly.
2. Add rose water a little at a time, beating constantly with a fork.
3. When cold cream is mixed thoroughly, pour into jars.

Rose Dusting Powder

1 cup unscented talc powder
1 cup cornstarch

½ teaspoon rose oil

1. Combine the talc and cornstarch thoroughly.
2. Stir in the oil. Let dry thoroughly and put in a tight-fitting container.

Harvests fresh from the garden are used to create products for hair and skin cleansing.

COOKING WITH ROSES

Rose petals and rose hips can be transformed into fascinating and even highly nutritious delicacies to eat or drink.

Most of us have to develop a taste for rose flavor. A little goes a long way, so it's a good idea to start sparingly. But the addition of rose petals or rose water can change a simple dish into an exotic taste treat.

Tips For Using Rose Petals In Recipes

1. Use only blossoms from plants that have not been treated with pesticides.
2. Select fragrant roses, preferably old-fashioned ones, because there is a relationship between fragrance and flavor.
3. Gently pull petals apart and cut the bitter white tips from the base of each petal.
4. Wash all petals before using.
5. To dry petals for later use, spread on a tray in a warm, arid place until brittle. Stir daily to prevent mildew. You can buy dried petals in organic food shops.
6. Ready-made rose water and rose syrup are available from some natural food shops and gourmet or international specialty stores.

Rose Petal Jam

1 pound fresh rose petals   1 pound sugar
2 pounds sugar   Juice of 1 lemon
Water

1. Pack petals tightly in a large jar or crock with alternating layers of sugar.
2. Pour enough hot water into jar to cover the petals. Cover with damp cloth for 3 days.
3. Then prepare a syrup, using enough water to dissolve 1 pound of sugar before it boils.
4. Cook to soft ball stage.
5. Cook this syrup with the petals and their juices.
6. Let simmer until the mixture is about the consistency of honey. Remove from the stove. Stir in lemon juice.
7. Pour into sterilized jars and seal.
Makes 3 to 4 pints.

Crystallized Rose Petals

Washed and dried rose petals   Granulated sugar
Egg white

1. Beat egg white to foam and brush it on both sides of petals with a small pastry brush or fingers. Both sides must be moist, but with no excess egg white remaining.
2. Shake granulated sugar on both sides and place carefully on a tray.
3. Dry in refrigerator or a cool room for several days.
Use petals to garnish cakes or eat them as candy.

Prickly red rose hips of English sweetbrier rose.

English Rose Wafers

1 cup granulated sugar	2 tablespoons rose water
1 cup butter	2 tablespoons sherry
1 teaspoon nutmeg	2 cups sifted flour
Pinch of salt	1 tablespoon caraway
2 eggs, well beaten	seed (optional)

1. Cream sugar and butter until fluffy. Add nutmeg and salt.
2. Mix eggs, rose water, and sherry. Add to butter mixture.
3. Add flour and mix well. Blend in caraway seed. Refrigerate until well chilled.
4. Work with small batches of the dough at a time. Roll very thin on a floured board. Cut as desired with cookie cutters.
5. Bake at 300°F. until golden brown, about 10 to 12 minutes.
Makes 6 to 7 dozen.
Note: They keep well for several months when stored in a cookie tin.

Rose Cake

Make as cupcakes or 3-layer cake.

1¾ cups cake flour	1¾ teaspoons double-acting
1 cup sugar	baking powder
½ cup soft butter	1 teaspoon rose water
2 eggs	¼ teaspoon grated lemon rind
½ cup milk	⅛ teaspoon nutmeg or mace
½ teaspoon salt	Rose petal jam

1. Sift flour and resift with sugar.
2. Add remaining ingredients and beat for 2 or 3 minutes.
3. Bake in greased pans in 350°F. oven for about 25 minutes.
4. When cakes have been in oven about 15 minutes, pull rack out and drop a little jam on top of each cupcake or spread on layer. Return to oven until done.
Frost with rose frosting if desired.

Rose Frosting

3 ounces cream cheese	1 teaspoon rose water
2½ cups sifted confectioners' sugar	Almonds or pistachio nuts,
1 tablespoon milk	finely chopped

1. Cream the cheese with milk. Add the sugar gradually, blending well.
2. Add rose water.
3. Spread on cake and sprinkle with nuts.

Rose Butter

Rose petals	Sweet butter, softened

1. Place a layer of butter in the bottom of a crock or jar.
2. Cover with a layer of petals. Continue to alternate layers of butter and petals.
3. Seal tightly and store in cool place or refrigerator for several days.
Blend together just before using. Use on muffins, biscuits, or sandwiches.

Rose Petal Tea

1 to 1½ teaspoons dried rose petals
or buds to *each* cup boiling water

1. Rinse teapot with boiling water to heat.
2. Place rose petals in dry teapot.
3. Add boiling water. Let steep for at least 3 minutes.
4. Strain and serve hot or iced with cream, honey, sugar, or lemon as desired.

The Fruit Of The Rose

Apples and peaches are members of the rose family, so it should not be surprising that the rose bears fruit, too. The fruit of the rose is the colorful hips. These nutritious little fruits have been used throughout history in medicinal concoctions and remedies.

During World War II, when England was without citrus fruits, it was discovered that wild rose hips contained about 24 to 36 times more vitamin C than equal portions of orange juice, and 60 times more of the vitamin than lemons.

Hips are also a rich source of vitamins A, B, E, K, and P, as well as salt, phosphorus, calcium, and iron. Probably no other food produced in the garden even approaches rose hips for concentrated food value.

Hips are produced after the petals fall. In order to have a crop of hips, leave the last blooms of the season on the bush. *Rosa rugosa* and other shrub species produce the most nutritious hips.

Slice the hip open to reveal seeds, which can be removed and discarded, or boiled and strained to secure their vitamin E.

Tips For Using Rose Hips In Recipes

1. Use home-grown hips that have not been treated with pesticides, or gather wild hips you know have not been sprayed.

2. Remove blossom ends, stems, and leaves after gathering hips. Wash carefully to remove any insect damage. Chill and store in airtight containers to prevent loss of vitamin C. Use quickly, as hips spoil rapidly.

3. To remove seeds from hips, cut the fruit in half and take out seeds, or make a hole in the top and insert a sharp knife to remove seeds.

4. Since the seeds are very rich in vitamin E, it is a good idea to grind them and boil in a little bit of water. Strain through a cloth and add in place of part of the liquid called for in recipes.

5. Vitamin C is easily destroyed by contact with copper or aluminum, so use only stainless steel knives, wooden spoons, and earthenware or china bowls when preparing rose hips. Cook in glass, stainless steel, or enamel saucepans. Always cook quickly and keep the pan covered. Stir the hips as little as possible.

6. Before drying rose hips, wash and clean them first. Remove seeds or leave in. If the weather is warm and dry, spread out on a screen rack until hips are leathery with no moisture left. If climate is cool or humid, dry the hips in a dehydrator. Dried hips can be purchased in organic food stores.

Rose Hip Tea

1 to 1½ teaspoons dried rose hips and seeds to *each* cup boiling water

Prepare like ordinary tea. See rose petal tea, page 130.

Rose Hip Jam

2 cups rose hips, cleaned   Sugar
2 cups water

1. Cook hips in water until tender, mashing fruit while cooking.
2. Push pulp through a fine sieve.
3. Add 1 cup sugar to each cup pulp.
4. Cook until pulp thickens to jam consistency.
5. Pour into sterilized jars and seal.

Rose Hip Syrup

Add a tablespoon of this highly concentrated vitamin source to breakfast juice each day or use in gelatin salads, sauces, or desserts.

Dried rose hips   Sugar
Water

1. Place hips in just enough water to cover. Soak overnight.
2. To each cup of hips and water add ¼ cup sugar. Cook slowly until tender (about 30 minutes).
3. Strain into jars or bottles. Refrigerate until used.

GLOSSARY AND FINAL NOTES

If you are a beginning gardener who wants to learn more about roses, this glossary can acquaint you with the terminology.

Bare root. Roses dug from commercial growing fields in late winter and early spring (wrapped to preserve moisture), and shipped to retail nurseries or directly to mail-order customers.

Basal break. A new cane or stem arising from the budhead tissue or bud at the base of an old cane.

Basal growth. The expanded ring of tissue at the base of a cane where it connects with the budhead or another cane.

Break. Any new growth from the buds.

Bud. Refers to (1) the unopened flower, or (2) the eyes on the cane at the nodes, base of the cane, or the budhead. The origin of all new replacement growth.

Budding. The process of propagating a new rose plant by taking a growth eye and grafting it to understock.

Budhead. The enlarged expanded growth from a single bud just above the crown where a hybrid or a different variety of rose was grafted.

Bud union. A suture line where the hybrid budhead joins the rootstock.

Cane. The main stem of the rose plant. It bears the leaves, flowers, and fruits (hips).

Candelabra. A strong, dominant cane with accelerated growth originating from the bud union, exploding into a "candelabra" of blooms.

Clippers. A short hand-tool that cuts from both sides with either curved or straight blades.

Corky layer. Tissue that extends beyond the skin of a cane, forming a thick, spongy layer (bark) over the outside of the stem.

Crown. The point where roots and stems join; or, an expanded and enlarged area that is more stem in character than root.

Cultivar. A plant that has been horticulturally derived in cultivation (by selection, mutation or hybridizing). Distinguished from a natural variety that occurs in the wild.

Disbudding. Thinning out flower buds to develop better quality in the remaining blooms.

Dog-leg. A cane that grows outward, then upward, in a deformed shape.

Dormant. The period when a plant rests and its growth processes slow down or almost stop. Begins as days grow shorter and temperatures begin to drop. Ends when the plant is exposed to higher temperatures for an extended number of hours and new growth starts.

The smooth, bright orange fruit of a hybrid tea rose. Below: Climbing roses can offer protection and privacy when trained against a fence.

Forked terminal. The end of a pruned cane with 2 smaller canes at its tip that extend in opposite directions from 1 or more joints.

Genus. A plant classification, ranking between a family and a species. Designated by Latin or Latinized and capitalized singular noun. Example: *Rosa.*

Hat-rack. The dead end or stub of a cane that has been cut between buds or above stem joints.

Hip. The fruit of the rose; a seed pod formed from pollinated flowers after the petals fade.

Hybrid. Offspring of two plants of different genetic backgrounds (i.e., different species or varieties).

Hybrid budhead. A growth that occurs where a hybrid variety has been budded to rootstock of another variety, seedling, or species plant.

Internode. The stem space between two joints, nodes, or buds.

Joint. Thickened areas on canes at which buds appear, and from which all replacement growth arises.

Jointed terminal. The end of a pruned cane, having a smaller cane attached to it by a joint and continuing away on an angle.

Leaf scar. A line extending around the cane and thickened just under the bud at the node of a stem where a leaf previously has been attached.

Lopper. Pruning shears with extended handles at least 20 inches long.

Mulch. Any material placed on the soil to conserve soil moisture, maintain a more even temperature, and aid in weed control.

Mutation. A change in a plant gene that produces a new variety differing from the parent. Usually called a "sport."

Node. A joint or point where a branch, bud, or leaf meets the stem from which it develops.

Old roses. Many species of roses and hybrids developed prior to the introduction of hybrid teas and floribundas. Quite a few still are available from specialized rose growers.

Patented. Referring to rose varieties protected by U.S. government patent, granting exclusive right for 17 years to the patent holder.

Pesticide. A substance (most often a chemical) used to control insects and rodents. Sometimes refers to weed killers as well.

Plethora. A superabundance of small, undersized, low-quality buds found crowded on twigs at the top of a rose cane where careless bloom cutting has been practiced.

Prickle. The thorn on a rose cane.

Pruning. Cutting back or cutting off part of a rose cane for better shape and more fruitful growth.

Replacement. A cane that grows from a bud, replacing or filling the area of old or dead canes that have been removed.

Root connections. Root attachments to the crown or to larger roots.

Roots. The underground part of the plant that extends from the crown.

Rootstock. A seedling or species plant that was rooted from a cutting and on which the hybrid is budded.

Sinkage. The tendency of the rose plant to sink below the surface of the soil so that the crown, rootstock, and budhead are all below the soil's surface.

Species. A group of plants that resemble each other closely and that interbreed freely. Designated by a Latin or Latinized uncapitalized noun or adjective in combination with the genus name. Example: *Rosa* (genus), *Rosa chinensis* (species).

Sport. See Mutation.

Standard. Any variety of rose plant grafted to a tall main stem. These plants are often referred to as tree roses.

Striations. Streaks or lines of corky tissue on old or mature canes, indicating that the blooming capacity is ended or near its end.

Stub. The remains of a cane that has been removed, leaving the basal attachment to the mother cane and a short part of the original cane.

Sucker. A shoot that arises from below the budhead, from the rootstock.

Systemic. A pesticide or fungicide that is absorbed into the system of a plant, causing the plant juice to become toxic to its enemies. Often combined with plant food.

Transverse cut. A crosswise cut made at right angles, to the direction of growth of a cane.

Twig. A small stem, often many-jointed, that grows laterally to a main cane of the rosebush.

Understock. The rose that supplies the rootstock onto which the hybrid is grafted. Rootstock and understock are often used interchangeably.

Variety. A naturally occurring subgroup of plants in a species (the lowest or final classification) with similar characteristics. Each variety within a species keeps the basic character of the species, but has at least one or more individual characteristics of its own.

Whorl. A circular arrangement of leaves, flowers, or branches that grow from a node on a stem or cane.

Winterize. To provide protection from the cold.

Winterkill. To kill by exposure to abnormal winter conditions.

Pink miniatures and floribundas are planted as companions to provide repeated bloom on several levels.

Keeping Up With The Roses

A good rosarian is never satisfied with the *status quo*; never rests on past accomplishments, no matter how many awards are on display; and never stops improving horticultural knowledge, regardless of how well the garden grows.

Each year, there's a wealth of new information to sort through: new varieties are introduced; changes are made in pest-control products; and new techniques and ideas are presented by both professional and amateur gardeners.

Just sorting out what's beneficial to you can become a time-consuming job. But a good rosarian will find the time to keep abreast of current developments. The best place to start is with the American Rose Society.

American Rose Society

The American Rose Society currently boasts more than 18,000 members (mostly amateurs), making it one of the largest special plant societies in the United States. There are more than 400 chapters and affiliated and associated local rose societies throughout the country. The ARS has permanent headquarters in Shreveport, Louisiana, located on a 118-acre park known as The American Rose Center. There, the ARS develops its extensive rose gardens.

The American Rose Society offers its members the following services:

The monthly *American Rose* magazine is the only periodical devoted exclusively to information on the culture, use, and history of roses. It is a must for anyone seriously involved with roses.

The *American Rose Annual* is a hard-bound book containing up-to-date scientific information on roses and rose growing, plus other articles of general interest to rose lovers. It has been published yearly since 1916.

ARS maintains a large mail-lending library of books on roses and related horticulture, and provides personal answers to individual rose-growing questions.

ARS maintains cooperative research programs on rose-growing problems at various colleges and experimental stations.

ARS holds two National Rose Meetings and Rose Shows each year, and offers assistance to district rose conferences and shows.

In cooperation with the districts, ARS conducts schools to train and accredit qualified rose-show judges, and establishes rules and regulations for conducting rose shows.

The Society also grants prizes and awards for outstanding achievements in rose work.

The International Horticultural Congress has delegated the ARS as the International Registration Authority for Roses. IRAR publishes monthly and annual lists of all new roses that are registered with it.

Hundreds of individual reports from all over the country are tabulated into an annual report of national ratings of all commercially available roses (see page 92). This *Handbook for Selecting Roses* is available to anyone at 35¢ per copy.

An annual tabulation of the cultivars that win awards at rose shows is printed.

ARS maintains its liaison with field societies and rosarians via strategically placed personnel called Consulting Rosarians. These individuals are available to help anyone with rose problems. A list is available from the Society.

ARS also offers rose-show supplies, books, program materials, and other data relevant to the complete operation of a rose society.

To start your membership in this active Society, send $18.00 ($15.00 if over 65) to American Rose Society, P.O. Box 30,000, Shreveport, LA 71130.

Starfire, a 1959 introduction and an All-America Rose Selection, whose color is described as "medium-red."

Cooperative Extension Service

Your County Agent or State University Cooperative Extension Service *may* offer bulletins on roses, with regionalized rose-growing tips. Call your agent or write the State Extension Office to see what's available. See next page for your state address.

The following are examples of some informative bulletins:
Roses in Arizona—A-30 (Arizona);
Rose Culture for Georgia Gardeners—B-671 (Georgia);
Roses: Selection and Planting—G6600 (10¢) (Missouri);
Successful Rose Culture—C200 (40¢) (North Carolina);
Roses for the Home—H & G #25 (New Hampshire);
Rose (Rosa) Disorder: Rust—A2536 (5¢) (Wisconsin).

Free Information From Suppliers

Catalogs and brochures on rose culture are available free of charge from many commercial rose growers and suppliers. Write for available information. See page 140 for addresses.

Recommended Reading

Anyone can Grow Roses
Dr. Cynthia Wescott (Collier)

Climbing Roses
Helen Van Pelt Wilson (M. Barrows)

History of the Rose
Roy E. Shepherd (Macmillan)

How to Grow Roses
Edited by Philip Edinger (Sunset Books)

How to Grow Roses
L. H. D. McFarland and Robert Pyle (Macmillan)

Modern Roses 7
(The McFarland Company)

Old Roses for Modern Gardens
Richard Thomson (D. Van Nostrand)

Rockwells' Complete Book of Roses
F. F. Rockwell and Esther C. Grayson (Doubleday)

Rose Recipes
Jean Gordon (Red Rose Publications)

Rose Recipes from Olden Times
Eleanour Sinclair Rohde (Dover Publications)

Roses
James Underwood Crockett (Time-Life Books)

Roses for Every Garden
R. C. Allen (M. Barrows)

Roses for Pleasure
Richard Thomson and Helen Van Pelt Wilson (D. Van Nostrand)

Shrub Roses for Every Garden
Michael Gibson (Collins)

The Book of Old Roses
Dorothy Stemler (Bruce Humphries Publishers)

The Dictionary of Roses in Color
S. Millar Gault and Patrick M. Synge (Madison Square Press)

The Magic World of Roses
Matthew A. R. Bassity (Hearthside Press)

The Old Shrub Roses
Graham Thomas (Phoenix House)

The Terrace Gardener's Handbook
Linda Yang (Doubleday)

Wild and Old Garden Roses
Gordon Edwards (Macmillan)

Handbook on Roses—$1.50 from
Brooklyn Botanic Gardens
1000 Washington Avenue
Brooklyn, NY 11225

A rose-lined front pathway makes for a warm welcome.

State Cooperative Extension Services

Alabama
Coop. Extension Service
Auburn University
Auburn, Al 38630

Alaska
Coop. Extension Service
University of Alaska
Fairbanks, AK 99701

Arizona
Coop. Extension Service
University of Arizona
Tucson, AZ 85712

Arkansas
Coop. Extension Service
University of Arkansas
Box 391
Little Rock, AR 72203

California
Public Service
University Hall
University of California
Berkeley, CA 94720

Colorado
Bulletin Room
Colorado State University
Fort Collins, CO 80521

Connecticut
Agricultural Publications
University of Connecticut
Storrs, CT 06268

Delaware
Mailing Room
Agricultural Hall
University of Delaware
Newark, DE 19711

Florida
Bulletin Room, Bldg. 440
University of Florida
Gainesville, FL 32601

Georgia
Coop. Extension Service
University of Georgia
Athens, GA 30601

Hawaii
Publications Distribution Office
Krass Hall
University of Hawaii
2500 Dole Street
Honolulu, HI 96822

Idaho
Mailing Room
Agricultural Science Bldg.
University of Idaho
Moscow, ID 83843

Illinois
Agricultural Publications Office
123 Mumford Hall
University of Illinois
Urbana, IL 61801

Indiana
Mailing Room
Agricultural Admin. Bldg.
Purdue University
West Lafayette, IN 47907

Iowa
Publications Distribution Center
Printing and Publications Bldg.
Iowa State University
Ames, IA 50010

Kansas
Distribution Center
Umberger Hall
Kansas State University
Manhattan, KS 66502

Kentucky
Bulletin Room
Experiment Station Bldg.
University of Kentucky
Lexington, KY 40506

Louisiana
Publications Librarian
Room 192, Knapp Hall
Louisiana State University
Baton Rouge, LA 70803

Maine
Department of Public Information
PICS Bldg.
University of Maine
Orono, ME 04473

Maryland
Agricultural Duplicating Services
University of Maryland
College Park, MD 20742

Massachusetts
Coop. Extension Service
Stockbridge Hall
University of Massachusetts
Amherst, MA 01002

Michigan
MSU Bulletin Office
Box 231
Michigan State University
East Lansing, MI 48823

Minnesota
Bulletin Room
Coffey Hall
University of Minnesota
St. Paul, MN 55101

Mississippi
Coop. Extension Service
Mississippi State University
State College, MS 39762

Missouri
Publications
B-9 Whitten Hall
University of Missouri
Columbia, MO 95201

Montana
Extension Mailing Room
Montana State University
Bozeman, MT 59715

Nebraska
Department of Information
College of Agriculture
University of Nebraska
Lincoln, NE 68503

Nevada
Agricultural Communications
University of Nevada
Reno, NV 89507

New Hampshire
Mail Service, Hewitt Hall
University of New Hampshire
Durham, NH 03824

New Jersey
Bulletin Clerk
College of Agriculture
Rutgers University
New Brunswick, NJ 08903

New Mexico
Bulletin Office
Dept. of Agricultural Information
Drawer 3A1
New Mexico State University
Las Cruces, NM 88001

New York
Mailing Room, Building 7
Research Park
Cornell University
Ithaca, NY 14850

North Carolina
Publications Office
Dept. of Agriculture Information
Box 5037—State College Station
North Carolina State University
Raleigh, NC 27607

North Dakota
Dept. of Agricultural Information
North Dakota State University
Fargo, ND 51802

Ohio
Extension Office
Ohio State University
2120 Fyffe Road
Columbus, OH 43210

Oklahoma
Central Mailing Services
Oklahoma State University
Stillwater, OK 74074

Oregon
Bulletin Mailing Service
Industrial Bldg.
Oregon State University
Corvallis, OR 97331

Pennsylvania
Sales Supervisor
230 Agriculture Admin. Bldg.
Pennsylvania State University
University Park, PA 16802

Rhode Island
Resource Information Office
16 Woodward Hall
University of Rhode Island
Kingston, RI 02881

South Carolina
Dept. of Agricultural Comm.
112 Plant and Animal Sci. Bldg.
Clemson University
Clemson, SC 29631

South Dakota
Agricultural Information Office
Extension Bldg.
South Dakota State University
Brookings, SD 57006

Tennessee
Agricultural Extension Service
University of Tennessee
Box 1071
Knoxville, TN 37901

Texas
Dept. of Agric.
Communications
Texas A&M University
College Station, TX 77843

Utah
Extension Publications Officer
Library 124
Utah State University
Logan, UT 84321

Vermont
Publications Office
Morrill Hall
University of Vermont
Burlington, VT 05401

Virginia
Extension Division
Virginia Polytechnic Institute
Blacksburg, VA 24061

Washington
Coop. Extension, Publications Bldg.
Washington State University
Pullman, WA 99163

West Virginia
Coop. Extension Service
West Virginia University
Morgantown, WV 26506

Wisconsin
Agricultural Bulletin Bldg.
1535 Observatory Drive
University of Wisconsin
Madison, WI 53706

Wyoming
Bulletin Room, College of Agriculture
University of Wyoming
Box 3354—University Station
Laramie, WY 82070

This old shrub rose has gone many seasons since it was last pruned—hence its mammoth size.

Catalog Sources

Burgess Seed and Plant Company (4)
Box 2000
Galesburg, MI 49053
This old established nursery offers some of the most popular roses.

W. Atlee Burpee Company (5)
Warminster, PA 18974
Their large catalog includes a few miniatures and shrub species, along with favorite hybrid teas and climbers.

Jackson and Perkins (8)
Medford, OR 97501
One of the world's largest rose growers offers a 40-page catalog, mostly of roses (all modern).

Farmer Seed and Nursery Company (9)
Faribault, MN 55021
A small selection of hybrid teas, including subzeroes, and floribundas. A few shrubs and climbers.

Henry Field Seed and Nursery Company (10)
Shenandoah, IA 51602
Miniatures and other modern classes, including subzero hybrids.

Gurney Seed and Nursery Company (12)
Yankton, SD 57078
Some old shrubs and the standard modern roses.

Earl May Seed and Nursery Company (18)
Shenandoah, IA 51603
Subzero roses and modern classifications; also products for growers.

Reuter Seed Company, Inc. (22)
P.O. Box 19255
New Orleans, LA 70179
A few popular rose varieties.

R. & H. Shumway, Seedsman (26)
628 Cedar St.
Rockford, IL 61101
Small collection of shrubs and modern roses.

Armstrong Nurseries, Inc. (55)
P.O. Box 4060
Ontario, CA 91762
One of the major suppliers. Offers a big colorful catalog of modern roses.

Arp Roses, Inc. (56)
P.O. Box 3338
Tyler, TX 75701
List of patented and nonpatented popular roses.

Buckley Nursery Company (57)
Buckley, WA 98321
List of modern roses, including trees.

Carroll Gardens (58)
P.O. Box 310
Westminister, MD 22157
Collection of modern rose classes.

Eastern Roses (60)
Box 203
West Long Branch, NJ 07764
List of imported varieties for gardeners with a gambling spirit. Small supply.

Roses by Fred Edmunds (61)
6235 S. West Kahle Road
Wilsonville, OR 97070
Will send a 24-page catalog of modern roses.

Emlong Nurseries Inc. (62)
Stevensville, MI 49127
Good selection of modern roses, including miniatures and shrubs.

Earl Ferris Nursery (63)
Hampton, IA 50441
Some shrubs and a collection of modern roses.

Inter-State Nurseries (65)
Hamburg, IA 51644
Good collection of modern roses.

Kelly Brothers Nurseries, Inc. (66)
Dansville, NY 14437
A few shrub and species roses.

Krider Nurseries, Inc. (69)
P.O. Box 69
Middlebury, IN 46540
Modern roses, including subzeroes, and a few old-fashioned and shrub roses.

Kroh Brothers Nursery (70)
P.O. Box 536
Loveland, CO 80537
Selected old favorites and new cultivars.

Lamb Nurseries (71)
E. 101 Sharp Avenue
Spokane, WA 99202
Their hardy perennial catalog includes miniature roses.

McDaniel's Miniature Roses (72)
7523 Zemco Street
Lemon Grove, CA 92045
List of miniature varieties.

Miniature Plant Kingdom (73)
4125 Harrison Grade Road
Sebastopol, CA 95472
Large selection of miniatures.

Mini-Roses (74)
P.O. Box 4255, Station A
Dallas, TX 75208
List of minatures available.

**Moore Miniature Roses
(Sequoia Nursery)** (75)
2519 East Noble Avenue
Visalia, CA 93277
Large selection of miniature varieties.

Nor'east Miniature Roses (76)
58 Hammond Street
Rowley, MA 01969
List of miniatures.

**Carl Pallek and Sons
Nurseries** (77)
Box 137
Virgil, Ontario, Canada L0S-1T0
List of popular and hard-to-find roses, including some shrubs.

**'Pixie Treasures'
Miniature Rose Nursery** (78)
4121 Prospect Avenue
Yorba Linda, CA 92686
Large selection of miniature roses.

Port Stockton Nursery (79)
2910 East Main
Stockton, CA 95250
List of modern roses.

Roseway Nurseries (80)
8766 NE Sandy Blvd.
Portland, OR 97220
Catalog of modern varieties.

Spring Hill Nurseries Company (81)
6523 N. Galena Rd.
Peoria, IL 61632
Small selection of hybrid teas, miniatures, and shrubs.

Stanek's Nurseries (82)
East 2929, 27th Avenue
Spokane, WA 99203
Modern cultivars, supplies, and a few shrubs.

**Stark Brothers Nurseries and Orchards
Company** (84)
Louisiana, MO 63353
Small selection of modern roses and shrubs.

Stern's Nurseries (85)
Geneva, NY 14456
Some shrubs. Also modern classes, including subzero hybrids.

Stocking Rose Nursery (86)
785 North Capitol Avenue
San Jose, CA 95133
Modern cultivars, including miniatures, and a few novelties.

P. O. Tate Nursery (87)
Route 3
Tyler, TX 75705
This old nursery offers popular modern cultivars.

Taylor Nurseries (88)
4647 Union Bay Place NE
Seattle, WA 98105
Roses are their specialty, although no current catalog is available. Write your request for variety.

Thomasville Nurseries, Inc. (89)
P.O. Box 7
Thomasville, GA 31792
A few old roses and a good selection of modern ones.

Roses of Yesterday and Today (90)
802 Brown's Valley Road
Watsonville, CA 95076
Roses of yesterday and some unusual modern varieties.

Melvin E. Wyant Rose Specialist, Inc. (92)
Johnny Cake Ridge, Route 84
Mentor, OH 44060
Both old-fashioned shrubs and modern varieties, including miniatures.

McConnell Nursery Co., Ltd. (93)
Port Burwell, Ontario, Canada N0J-1T0
Modern roses, including some hard-to-find ones and a few shrubs.

Tiny Petals Nursery
489 Minot
Chula Vista, CA 92010
Miniature roses.

A close-up view of what many feel is the most beautiful flower in any garden: form, color and fragrance are the winning qualities of the rose.

Index

Page numbers in italics indicate illustrations.